Praise for *52 Leadership*

"With *52 Leadership Lessons*, John Parker Stewart delivers powerful, impactful insights into the mysteries of leadership and all its complex dimensions. John has the uncanny skill of revealing what few are even able to articulate about leadership. His stories and analogies are simply unforgettable. This book contains a wealth of valuable truths. Anyone reading it will quickly understand the brilliance and practicality of John's teachings."

TOM LEAVITT, former senior executive, leadership and organization development, Lockheed, Toshiba, Unocal, and NationsBank

"Parents around the world use stories to teach their children how to be better people. As a world-class executive coach, John Parker Stewart uses the power of fifty-two great stories of nature, history, and business to portray to us a new model that forms the pillars of leadership—creating purpose, delivering excellence, developing self and others, and leading change. *52 Leadership Lessons* is a stimulating and entertaining handbook for those who are in search of excellence in their personal and business lives."

IRENE LEUNG, CEO, Senior Citizen Home Safety Association, Hong Kong

"John Parker Stewart pulls from over three decades of experience leading leaders in some of the world's most effective companies. The wonderful feature of *52 Leadership Lessons* is that it's a book you CAN put down ... and then pick up again, and again, and again! It illuminates the subject by creating mental images that are each a little stand-alone epiphany on leadership. They are assimilated quickly, understood at a visceral level, and retained. Each story is preceded by a list of related leadership topics, and followed immediately by a brief set of considerations for its application. Busy execs will find this book to be a treasure."

JAMES C. ADAMSON, US Army colonel; former NASA space shuttle astronaut; former chief operations officer, United Space Alliance; former president, Lockheed Engineering and Sciences; former president, Honeywell TSI

"John Parker Stewart is a master at helping his clients discover their 'inner leaders' through humor and analogy. His *52 Leadership Lessons* resonate with all of us and keep teaching long after they're told."

BETH BRITT, retired vice president, change management and communications, Duke Energy

"*52 Leadership Lessons* is a must-read for all managers who wish to continually improve their management skills. It is an extremely compelling and timely book on leadership. John has successfully condensed over thirty years of executive training and coaching to provide valuable insight. Through stories that illustrate the various characteristics of effective leadership and execution of team dynamics, he provides practical direction necessary to succeed in today's competitive marketplace. I highly recommend this book to anyone who is interested in improving team leadership."

BRAD WHITWORTH, health and safety process manager, United Parcel Service

"I have been using the ideas and stories from John's teachings within product development teams for over twenty-five years. I also leaned heavily on these stories and insights while earning my MBA in technology management. John's insight into the basics of team management and human psychology are beautifully represented in easy-to-understand and, more importantly, easy-to-incorporate lessons. It is wonderful to finally have a book that puts some of John's powerful and entertaining stories into one volume. I highly recommend 52 *Leadership Lessons* to anyone who is leading any kind of team: work, sports, youth groups, volunteer groups, and even families."

BRIAN K. HOVIK, certified metalworking fluid management specialist and senior research and development engineer, Boeing

"Some say teaching is best done through the telling of stories. That certainly applies to how one learns the essence of leadership. In his 52 *Leadership Lessons*, John Parker Stewart has captured the best of the stories he has shared with audiences around the world. As I read them in this book, I find I enjoy and learn from them as much as I did when John first told them to me in person when he taught and coached me. They never get old and never lose their value or meaning."

KENNETH S. REIGHTLER JR., former astronaut and space shuttle pilot; former president, Lockheed Martin Space Operations

Other books in the Stewart Leadership Series

LEAD NOW!
A Personal Leadership Coaching
Guide for Results-Driven Leaders

52 Leadership Gems
Practical and Quick Insights for Leading Others

52
LEADERSHIP
LESSONS

Timeless Stories for
the Modern Leader

JOHN PARKER STEWART

PAGE TWO

Cataloguing in publication information is available
from Library and Archives Canada.
ISBN 978-1-77458-220-6 (paperback)
ISBN 978-1-77458-221-3 (ebook)

Page Two
pagetwo.com

Proofread by Steph VanderMeulen
Cover design by Peter Cocking
Interior design by Setareh Ashrafologhalai

stewartleadership.com
LEAD NOW!™ is a registered trademark of Stewart Leadership LLC.

*To my talented wife, Debra, who wrote the
first draft of many of these stories: I love
your gift of expression and your love of learning.*

Contents

Introduction

"Wisdom begins in wonder."

SOCRATES

WE LOVE stories! We have since we were small. Stories capture our interest, draw us in, and often teach us things we could learn in no other way.

The quotation at the top of the page, "Wisdom begins in wonder," is the essence of this collection of leadership lessons. Stories kindle our childlike curiosity and nudge us to learn by engaging our wonder. Stories, or analogies, have the potential to teach powerful lessons.

Over the years, I have had a special appreciation for stories that illustrate a vivid point in the field of management, leadership, and life in organizations—especially when the stories are the result of some strange or unusual aspect of life. I particularly enjoy vignettes from nature or history.

The analogies may be drawn from some vital aspect to the life of a plant, the daily routines of an animal, or the innovative discovery of a product or new procedure. These stories are both interesting and applicable in most cultures and societies, and consequently are easily used in large or small classroom settings.

For the past thirty-plus years of teaching professionals from all varieties of backgrounds around the globe, I have used these stories to make a point or teach a valuable principle. They often elicit an audible "Aha" from the audience as I share them, because usually the story is known to them, but the application is not.

It finally occurred to me to publish a volume that would make these stories available to you, the reader. Each is followed by a handful of questions or coaching tips for you to consider. Here are fifty-two of my favorite stories. Enjoy!

PART I

THE LEAD NOW! LEADERSHIP DEVELOPMENT MODEL

ECOMING AN AGILE, flexible leader requires easily accessible leadership development tools. While partnering with countless corporate and government organizations for over three decades, I've recognized a great need for such a toolkit.

In collaborating with over 10,000 busy supervisors, managers, directors, senior executives, presidents, and CEOs in corporations, and military officers, including generals, I've observed their desire—and struggle—to drive better results while meeting the everyday demands and goals of their respective positions. Part of their challenge was a lack of clear definition and processes to follow for their leadership development. Consequently, at Stewart Leadership we developed the LEAD NOW! Leadership Development Model, a simple, comprehensive framework that helps leaders develop the tools they need to assess and improve their ability to lead and coach others at a moment's notice.

The LEAD NOW! Leadership Development Model is a user-friendly, complete action guide for leaders at every level of the organization. It is built on the assumption that all leaders must achieve aligned and positive results—with their people and in their business—from both a marketplace (external) and an organizational (internal) perspective. This model is composed of Leadership Quadrants supported by 21 Leadership Dimensions that provide the basis for in-depth leadership skill building and action planning. A successful leader builds capability in all the quadrants. The quadrants and their respective dimensions are discussed more fully below.

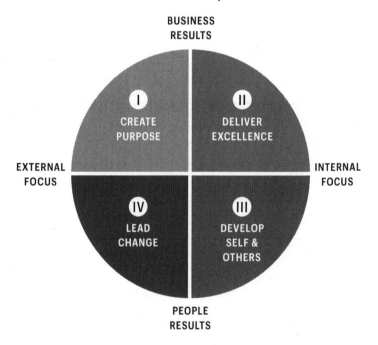

Quadrant I: Create Purpose (Externally Focused Business Results)

A leader is responsible for defining the group's vision and strategy. Creating purpose means identifying what the organization stands for, what it is going to do, why it needs to be done, and how it is positioned in the marketplace. This involves studying the competition, analyzing industry trends, thoroughly knowing the customer, and communicating effectively.

Quadrant I: Dimensions

The dimensions that allow you to create purpose are:

* **Customer Focus:** Deliver your product or service in such a way that you fulfill the needs, wants, and values of your customer better than anyone else.

* **Effective Communication:** Express an intended message, through the correct medium, in a manner that the recipient of the message will understand.

* **Presentation Skills:** Effectively communicate ideas to large or small audiences.

* **Strategic Thinking:** Balance short- and long-term actions to optimize business results.

Quadrant II: Deliver Excellence (Internally Focused Business Results)

A leader must deliver operational excellence—translating the strategy into day-to-day execution for the organization. Delivering excellence means ensuring that metrics are clear and deliverables are accomplished. This involves clear decision making, building consistent and measurable processes, continual improvement, and behaving with integrity.

Quadrant II: Dimensions

The dimensions that allow you to deliver excellence are:

- **Decision Making:** Understand not only why a decision needs to be made but also how to define, analyze, reach, and implement the decision, while communicating with those who will be affected by its outcomes.

- **Delegating:** Assign and communicate a task so that the individual understands the objective and timeline, is provided resources to complete the task, and knows you will support and not abandon or take over the task.

- **Dependability:** Receive an assignment and consistently follow through and deliver on the expected results.

- **Focusing on Results:** Focus on the desired outcome with precision and conviction.

- **Personal Integrity:** Demonstrate consistent honesty and commitment to your word.

- **Problem Solving:** Define and analyze a problem to deliver a high-quality solution with appropriate buy-in.

Quadrant III: Develop Self and Others (Internally Focused People Results)

Leaders must value learning for themselves and for others. Developing self and others means spending time building the talent on their teams, coaching others effectively, and staying current on professional and industry advances. This involves seeking personal improvement opportunities, managing their time, managing their egos, honing technical expertise, building and managing team dynamics, and coaching and developing others.

Quadrant III: Dimensions

The dimensions that allow you to develop yourself and others are:

- **Coaching:** Guide an individual to achieve improved performance through self-discovery, feedback, encouragement, and skill development.

- **Ego Management:** Develop a balanced level of confidence in your own skills, tools, judgment, and experience.

- **Listening:** Understand the intended message while having an awareness of the attitudes and feelings of others.

- **Personal Development:** Pursue the continual improvement of your abilities and knowledge.

- **Team Building:** Help a group of individuals work together to accomplish a common goal.

- **Time Management:** Plan and control how you spend the hours in your day to accomplish your goals and meet deadlines.

- **Valuing Others:** Recognize the potential within others and let them know that their capabilities, experience, and contributions are important.

Quadrant IV: Lead Change
(Externally Focused People Results)

A leader is responsible for creating and championing change that will benefit the organization. Leading change means understanding the broader marketplace and engaging and unifying others to create sustainable growth. This involves encouraging innovation, sponsoring change projects, influencing key decision makers, empowering stakeholders, managing resistance, and making change stick.

Quadrant IV: Dimensions

The dimensions that allow you to lead change are:

* **Change Management:** Communicate a compelling vision, lead minor and major changes within an organization, and sustain the change over time.

* **Innovation:** Apply new and better solutions to current or future needs.

* **Inspiring Commitment:** Earn the hearts and minds of the people with whom you associate.

* **Organizational Savvy:** Know how to get things done through formal and informal channels.

The Four Relationships

ONE OF the most powerful aspects of the LEAD NOW! Model is how each axis describes the needs of the four critical relationships of a leader. Tailoring your communication based on the needs of the person with whom you are interacting will help you build stronger rapport in the four key relationships that a leader needs to be successful.

Boss → Business results (revenue, expenses, punctuality, quality)

Direct Reports → People results (engagement, career development, team dynamics)

Peers → Internal focus (resource allocation, budget, process handoffs)

Customers → External focus (customer needs, competitive analysis, market trends)

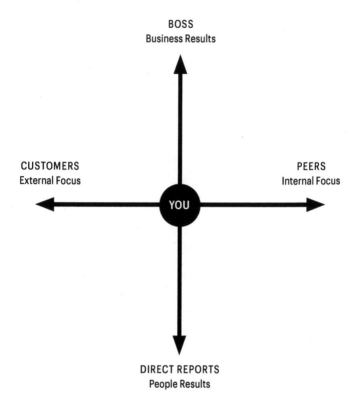

Business Results

To build a relationship with your boss and upper management, use the language of business results. Your boss is focused on results and is expecting you to deliver them. Business results are primarily what your boss is evaluated on. You will want to convey how you will achieve these results in your communication with your boss.

People Results

To build a relationship with your direct reports, use the language of people results. Direct reports are focused on how the dynamics of the team are going, the level of engagement, how they are being developed, and how talent is being promoted in the team.

Internal Focus

To build a relationship with your peers, use the language of internal focus. Peers are concerned with how resources are being allocated and how work is being done internally. Building effective relationships with peers is about managing these resources and the day-to-day work.

External Focus

To build a relationship with your customers, use the language of external focus. This concerns the broader marketplace in identifying the competitive landscape, industry trends, and current and future customer needs. This is focused on building effective relationships with key stakeholders outside of the organization.

It is essential that you understand the language, and establish and maintain each relationship for balanced performance. The LEAD NOW! Model teaches a leader what the four critical relationships are, and how to build them to accomplish the needed business results and people results.

The Personal Development Process
Five Steps to Sustain Personal Change

O VER THE YEARS, I have witnessed countless attempts by professionals from all walks of life to change some aspect of their behavior in leading others. Studying why some have failed while others have succeeded reveals tremendously helpful insights. The difference between the two has led us to develop a simple and practical five-step model that can be followed by anyone who desires sustained personal change in any aspect of life.

Following all five of these steps will help anyone sustain personal behavior change. The trick is making sure you do all five steps. Leaving out any single step, especially the last one, can dramatically decrease your chance of sustained behavioral change.

Here are the steps.

1 Awareness
2 Desire

3 New resources and skills
4 Action
5 Support

To illustrate the power of these steps, let us use the example of someone who wants to lose weight.

Step 1: Awareness

You realize you are not in the physical shape you think you should be in. Maybe you read an article on health, went to the doctor, or looked at other people's bodies at the beach. Another way of understanding this first critical step is to substitute the term "awareness" with "aha." It is the lightbulb of a new idea, fact, or impression that hits you as a result of feedback from another person (a friend, coach, mentor, or family member) or a personal discovery.

If you want to, you can move on to the next step, but only if you really want to. If there is no interest in moving to Step 2, then the potential for change stops at this first step.

Step 2: Desire

You desire to do something with this new awareness or aha. You want to do something about it because you are dissatisfied with the current status. You do not want to be overweight. You do not like the way your clothes fit. You do not like the fact that you are out of shape. This is about personal motivation to do something about your awareness or the knowledge you have gained.

If you want to, you can move on to the next step, but only if you really want to. Otherwise, the change process stops right at this point.

Step 3: New Resources and Skills

Once you are aware and want to change, it is necessary to get the resources and skills to prepare you for action. You need to understand how to read food labels, what are the pros and cons of various dieting approaches, and what exercises would be helpful for you. This is when training and tools become so important, so you can learn new skills and get the ability to help you turn your desire into action.

Step 4: Action

Now that you are armed with awareness, desire, and new resources and skills, you are prepared to put these tools to work for you. The action step is where the rubber meets the road. Set reasonable goals that encourage. Use the new resources. Start making small changes.

Unfortunately, this is the step where change often fizzles out. Despite the successful completion of all the other previous steps, this step can begin with a bang and too often end with a whimper. People are not able to stick with it. They become discouraged. They allow old habits to take over. The needs of the day soon dominate and little is changed. Without the last step, Step #5, the likelihood of sustained change is considerably lower. The key to SUSTAINED personal change is in the final step.

Step 5: Support

No matter how strong-minded we are, there will come a point where we need the encouragement of others to help us continue. Sharing your goal or commitment with a trusted friend, asking them to keep you on track, will be the final piece of the formula for personal success. In those moments of weakness or discouragement, your supportive associate will kindly yet firmly watch out for you, encourage you, and provide the support over time that you seek. When this final step is ignored, the longevity of your goal is jeopardized. Including this final step makes all the difference in the world for you to accomplish the change you desire.

Yet, support is not just an individual-to-individual activity. Having personal or group support is just one kind of support. The other type of support is organizational or structural. This involves the support from policies, procedures, and rules of the organization you work for or the structure of your habits and friends. For example, it is very smart to join a weight loss support group. It is also smart to change the contents of your cupboards at home and change the position of your La-Z-Boy recliner so it isn't directed toward the TV.

One of our goals in writing this book is to increase your awareness, prompt your desire, provide you with tools and resources, give you specific actions to take, and offer ideas for support to help you on your leadership journey! So, where should you start? Good question. Let's talk about how to develop yourself as a leader.

Turning Your
Insights into Action
Developing Your
Leadership Capabilities

T O HELP you develop your own leadership capabilities, at the beginning of each chapter, each Leadership Lesson is referenced to applicable leadership dimensions in the LEAD NOW! Model. You can focus on the particular Lesson that will be the most helpful to your individual development needs. For example, if you need specific help with delegating or innovation, you can pay particular attention to the Lessons that apply to those dimensions.

You may be asking yourself, which leadership dimension should I focus on? Below are three questions to help you identify which dimensions and Lessons you should focus on to add the greatest value to you in your leadership journey today.

As you review the 21 Leadership Dimensions in the LEAD NOW! Model, ask yourself these three questions (we also strongly encourage you to complete the online LEAD NOW! Self-Assessment for additional insight—go to stewartleadership .com for more information).

1 Which dimensions do I like doing the most and the least?

2 Which dimensions are my most and least effective?

3 Which dimensions are most relevant to my current or future job?

Based on the answers to these questions, which dimensions stand out? Can you identify one or two that would provide the biggest benefit in your effort to accomplish business and people results today?

As you select one or two dimensions to focus on, look through the table of contents for Gems that will help inspire you, provide coaching guidance, and that you could share with your team to support your leadership development.

As an additional resource for your personal leadership growth, we recommend that you use the other two books in the Stewart Leadership Series, *LEAD NOW! A Personal Leadership Coaching Guide for Results-Driven Leaders* and *52 Leadership Gems: Practical and Quick Insights for Leading Others.*

All three books in the Stewart Leadership Series are aligned with the LEAD NOW! Model and will support your development. *LEAD NOW!* provides scores of coaching tips for each dimension, and *52 Leadership Lessons* provides inspirational stories organized by each dimension. Of course, *52 Leadership Gems* provides time-tested wisdom. Together, these three resources summarize some of the greatest leadership thinking that has emerged over the past thirty years and put it together for easy and instant application.

PART II

THE 52 LEADERSHIP LESSONS

Lesson 1
Baboons and Impalas

Related Leadership Dimensions
Team Building
Valuing Others
Focusing on Results
Innovation
Dependability

ATURE CAN BE a unique matchmaker. Baboons and impalas may not seem to have much in common, or much to offer each other, but they are actually a perfect fit. Baboons are innately hyper-alert and their vision and ability to climb trees for a better vantage point make them ideal "watchmen." Impalas stir up bugs and insects as they graze, making it much easier for baboons to gather meals. These two species are frequently seen grazing together because each provides a vital service to the other.

Likewise, antelopes live with oxpeckers, tiny birds that shriek to warn the antelopes of danger in exchange for being able to feed on the insect larvae that cluster on the antelopes' skin. The sea anemone rides on the back of the hermit crab, whose mobility brings food to the anemone while its stingers help protect the crab from predators.

Who would ever have thought that animals so different from one another could team up so effectively?

Like these animals, people have many differences. But unlike the animals described here, people often allow differences to separate them from others. We all have a tendency to prefer similarities in those we work with, and we would rather avoid those who are different from us. Too few of us have caught on to the natural synergistic potential of capitalizing on symbiotic differences. Many of us tend to condemn others for their weaknesses instead of appreciating their strengths.

The antelope does not distrust the oxpecker, nor does the hermit crab resent carrying the full weight of the sea anemone. The baboon does not criticize the impala for having poor vision. Yet how often do we distrust people because they are different? Do we ever resent carrying the full weight of our boss, forgetting the benefits that come to us as a result? Do we tend to focus on differences as weaknesses instead of strengths?

Viewing people's differences from us in a favorable light allows us to see significant untapped advantages for ourselves and others. When alliances develop, we call it teamwork. And in the organizations that have it, one plus one equals three... or even more!

Application

A few tips:

1 No one possesses every skill or capability. We are all a blend of talents and weaknesses.

2 Recognize in your associates the strengths that they bring to projects and assignments.

3 Consider how your own strengths can counter some of your team's deficiencies.

4 When selecting others to be on a team with you, choose those unlike you. A healthy blend of attributes and capabilities will bring balance to the team and lead to more productive outcomes.

Do we tend to focus on weaknesses instead of strengths? Do we see differences as barriers?

Lesson 2
Prescribed Burns

Related Leadership Dimensions
Change Management
Personal Development
Focusing on Results
Strategic Thinking

FOR THE PAST 100 years, we have carefully watched and patrolled the earth's forests to prevent forest fires from destroying our national parks. The ugliness of raging fires leaves the land scarred and black. We have done our job well—perhaps too well.

A walk through a healthy forest will reveal a heavy blanket of debris and plant life. Trees reach to the sky; they're in abundance, almost blocking the sun from the forest floor. It seems peaceful, beautiful, and quiet. But it is a bit too quiet, according to forest rangers.

Because we have carefully guarded the forest from fires, we have tipped nature's scale into an unfavorable balance. Without fires periodically cleaning out excess plant life and removing dead debris, there is no longer a natural way of maintaining nature's delicate balance. First, as the shade-loving plants increase, they create a thick bed that prevents the penetration of seeds needed for future tree growth. Second, if too many tall trees are growing, they block out the life-giving light necessary for the sun-loving plants below. Not only do we have an extreme fire hazard created by the excess debris, but we lose vital plant growth. To solve this problem, forest rangers have introduced prescribed burns.

As an area of the forest becomes too cluttered and dangerous, a controlled fire is created to burn out the unwanted debris and plant life. It is done with prescribed conditions only after careful study, monitoring, and site preparation. First, it must be done either in late spring or in early fall after a rainfall. Second, the degree of heat must be hot enough to considerably set back unwanted growth, but not so hot as to damage the big trees. Third, an additional fire is set to remove the burned residue. Fourth, the area is then watched and monitored to determine growth progress.

The short-term effects of a fire are not aesthetically pleasing, but the long-term result is beneficial and even necessary. New growth softens the initial harshness of the fire. Without these prescribed burns, the whole forest would deteriorate and eventually cease to exist.

This analogy applies to our lives. Businesses, as well as relationships, need careful monitoring to ensure constant growth. Being open to ridding ourselves of excess "debris" and moving ahead is a healthy approach to any endeavor. If we are bogged down in heavy debris, we might be choking out the very things we need to maintain a healthy environment.

Consider your organization, business, and relationships. Is it time, perhaps, for a "prescribed burn" to restore balance and promote vital growth?

Application

Examine your business, relationships, and organization. Ask yourself:

1 How do you allocate your resources? Are they providing you what you expected and what you need?

2 Are you getting bogged down by any "debris" (procedures, red tape, needless meetings, and negative relationships) that stifles other opportunities?

3 Do you feel you have an appropriate balance that promotes healthy growth?

It is healthy to periodically remove excesses to restore balance and promote growth in our lives.

Lesson 3
Employees Are Like Turtles

Related Leadership Dimensions
Delegating
Coaching
Inspiring Commitment
Team Building
Focusing on Results

W HAT HAPPENS when fear permeates an organization? Consider a turtle scrunched safely inside its shell. When it is hungry or thirsty, it must move. This requires that part of its body must exit its safe home. First it pokes its nose—just barely—outside the shell and looks around. As soon as it feels it is relatively safe, the rest of its head and long neck slowly and cautiously emerge. It looks around again—moving its neck from side to side—just to make sure all appears safe, then the feet come out, and it slowly starts walking along.

But whack its head once, just once—even lightly—and what happens? Instant retreat back into its shell where it remains, doing nothing! After a while, the entire process repeats itself, but this time the turtle is even more reluctant because the whack it received left a strong and lasting impression.

Now, here's the question: How many factories and offices are littered with "turtle shells" just sitting there, filled with fear, doing the absolute minimum because they have been whacked on their heads one too many times?

Is your organization suffering from "turtle syndrome"? In an environment of fear, employees retreat into their shells. Productivity suffers. Innovation and creativity die. Morale tanks. The fear may come from a supervisor or it may be a negative cultural influence permeating the organization.

Give your employees the opportunity to stick their necks out without getting "whacked." Let them suggest improvements. Avoid condemning new or unusual ideas.

Be especially careful when giving negative feedback. Consider first-time mistakes as opportunities for learning. Build an environment where risk-taking is encouraged instead of immediately rejected.

Don't let unbridled zeal to meet a target lead to an organization full of turtle shells. Earn your people's loyalty and unlock their productivity. Replace their fear with trust.

Application

Here are a few points for reflection.

1 Are you aware of managers who intimidate or supervise through fear? Their success is very limited.

2 Consider your own leadership style. How does it influence your team's productivity?

3 How willing are your people to suggest improvements? That is a direct indicator of the amount of fear in your organization.

Give your employees the opportunity to stick their necks out without getting whacked.

Lesson 4
Vision in the Fog

Related Leadership Dimensions
Focusing on Results
Problem Solving
Change Management
Coaching
Innovation

O N THE FOURTH of July in 1952, Florence Chadwick attempted to swim the saltwater channel from Catalina Island to the California coast, a distance of twenty-six miles.

Florence had several dangerous enemies. One was the cold water. But she was no stranger to the cold. She had already crossed the bone-chilling English Channel in both directions. Another challenge was the sharks, which had to be driven away with rifle shots. But on that particular morning, Florence had a far more daunting enemy.

After fifteen hours in the water, a thick fog set in. Despite all her experience and training, Florence began to doubt her ability. The fog had a demoralizing effect on her. She swam for another hour and then asked to be taken out of the water. Sitting in the boat, she learned that she had stopped swimming just one mile from the coast. She had covered twenty-five miles, but the disorienting blanket of fog defeated her.

Later, she said, "If I could have seen land, I might have made it." She was not beaten by fatigue, by cold, or even sharks. She was beaten by the fog. Why? Because she couldn't see her goal.

Two months later, Chadwick made another attempt. The same thick fog set in, but this time was different. Florence succeeded in reaching the coastline. What made the difference? Florence said that she kept a mental image of the shoreline in her mind, which helped her ignore the thick fog, maintain her focus, and reach her goal.

Have you ever noticed that the greatest burst of energy comes when a runner rounds the corner and sees the finish line, or when the athlete looks at the clock and sees only seconds remaining in the match or game?

It is the same in life. When we are weary from the struggle, it is often because we have lost sight of our goal. We no longer see how our day-to-day activities are connected to achieving our big goals. It is easy to get lost in the fog of daily minutiae. Define your goal and stay focused. Anticipate barriers, challenges, and unpleasant surprises. Don't get discouraged. Allow yourself to succeed by keeping the big picture in your mind, and do not get bogged down by daily tasks. Stay true to the course and you will reach your target even when it is obscured and seems impossible.

Application

A few tips:

1 As you consider improving some aspect of your life, set a clearly defined target so you know where you are going.

2 Recognize and accept that you will encounter barriers and opposition in your journey. Prepare for them the best you can by mitigating risks and distractions.

3 Make certain you are able to visualize what victory looks like. This will keep you going as you meet all types of resistance. Let this mental picture fuel your drive.

Do not let the fog of daily minutiae obscure the grandeur of your goal.

Lesson 5
How to Train Your Killer Whale

THE TRAINER stands on the nose of the killer whale and, together, they dive to the bottom of the pool. The trainer moves her feet to the whale's flippers and holds on to the large nose. They come up out of the water and shoot twenty-five to thirty feet into the air. It's a show-stopping performance. The crowd knows it is seeing something truly awesome. Describing this particular trick, the Rocket Hop, the trainer says, "It's pretty much the coolest feeling ever." What did it take to get that trainer and that killer whale to the point of being able to perform such stunts together? A lot.

First of all, new trainers go through up to three years of careful training before they ever get into the water with one of the massive twenty-six-foot-long, six-ton whales. Even at that point, before the actual training begins, trainers get to know the whale and form a relationship. They develop an understanding and fondness for each other. They trust each other. Trainers describe it as a step-by-step sequence that cannot be rushed.

The most important part of this process is daily interaction between the trainer and the whale. Trainers take part in "relationship sessions" with the whale. They spend one-on-one time together: They look into the whale's eyes, rub its skin, play with it, and sometimes they simply swim together, sharing quiet time. What they do is not as important as just being together. Once trainers have bonded with the whales, they follow a careful training program, gradually teaching the whales to perform tricks that delight audiences. Throughout the entire process, and even after the whale is completely trained, personal interaction with the whale is crucial and must be maintained.

How much time do you spend with your people? Just like whales, they need to understand you and trust you. Get out of your office, and let them get to know you. Find out what's important to them. And don't take a big stick with you. Remember the whale trainer's philosophy: When you need someone to perform, you must first build a rapport that leads to mutual trust.

Motivating employees requires an investment of time. You can't rush the process of establishing trust. Let them know you are genuinely interested in them. Reassure them that you mean them no harm, but are seeking what is in their best interest. People don't care how much you know, until they know how much you care.

Application

Here are some points for reflection.

1 Consider the amount of time you spend with each of your people. What messages do you send when you are with them?

2 Do you sense there is trust between the two of you? Once you have trust, their response to your requests will be more favorable.

3 To maintain this level of relationship requires an ongoing investment of time, patience, and interest. How much are you investing?

People, like whales, won't perform for you until you have built a relationship of mutual trust.

Lesson 6
Hooks and Loops

Related Leadership Dimensions
Innovation
Problem Solving
Personal Development
Change Management

WHEN RETURNING from a long hike in the woods, it is common to discover that your clothes have carried home little pieces of nature—those prickly, sticky, terribly hard-to-get-off things called burrs. They are anything but a delight, and are clearly an annoyance—unless you are George de Mestral.

On a hunting trip, George and his dog returned from the woods covered in burrs. He was curious about how these annoying things were able to cling so effectively to his clothes and his dog's fur. He examined one of them under a microscope and discovered hooks that clung to the tiny loops of the fabric of his clothes. He was struck by the idea that he could mimic this hook and loop approach to create a new type of fastener.

His idea was not taken seriously by most. In fact, he was often laughed at as he tried to find support for his idea. But he knew his idea had potential, so he persisted.

He was able to convince a French weaver to help him develop a process that imitated the hook and loop style of the burr. Using a cotton fabric, they developed a two-part fastener. On one side were hooks and on the other side loops. It worked quite well except for one problem—the fabric wore out too quickly.

He was discouraged and ridiculed, but George de Mestral did not give up. Years passed and he still had not discovered a fabric that would hold up to the constant pull he needed to duplicate the tenacity of the burr. Finally, after treating nylon with infrared light, he had his fabric.

Mass production was the next step. Through diligent research and effort, and with the help of his weaver friend, the answers were found and production began. After a decade of work and persistent effort, a revolutionary type of fastener was now available. Combining the words "velvet" and "crochet" formed the name of his new product—you know what it is. Think of all the uses it has in your life.

We are continuously faced with opportunities disguised as insoluble problems. Whether we view them as opportunities or challenges is our choice. Just as George de Mestral found good qualities in an annoyance, let's open our minds and look for windows of opportunity.

Application

Here are some points for reflection.

1 Ponder some of the annoyances you face. See if you can break them down to better understand them. What ideas emerge as you identify the smaller parts?

2 Notice the patient persistence that George employed to finally succeed in the production of his product.

3 When pursuing a dream, it is rare to go it alone. George de Mestral sought help from someone who had expertise he lacked. What help do you need in order to resolve your challenge? Who is best qualified to help you?

We are continuously faced with opportunities disguised as insoluble problems.

Lesson 7
Chains and Ribbons

Related Leadership Dimensions
Inspiring Commitment
Innovation
Valuing Others
Change Management
Team Building

N THE EARLY part of the last century, circuses and zoos
employed a certain method of training for elephants. They
were bound by a heavy chain and tethered to a sturdy post.
Initially, when the elephants were young and small, they
could never break the chain—but that did not stop them from
trying. However, they soon resigned themselves to the fact that
the pull of the chain on their legs meant they could not move.

As the elephants grew older, however, they could easily
have broken the chains but they no longer tried. They were

conditioned, when young, to believe that they were bound by chains much stronger than the elephants were. In fact, after years of having the chain on its hind leg, an elephant did not break away no matter how gentle the pull—even when the chain was replaced by a piece of rope, string, or even ribbon, the elephant did not break it. It became so accustomed to the chain that when it felt the tug of the tether, it went no farther.

Such treatment is no longer used because of its cruel nature. But the basic principle of this training—conditioning—is still very prevalent in our world, and it is sometimes unconsciously done. Employees are susceptible to it, just like elephants. If we chain our people down, they become conditioned to the restraint, and eventually their innovation, creativity, and self-motivation die.

Then, down the road those chains may be removed, but the conditioning influence remains. You may tap into your employees' resourcefulness and innovation—only to find that they are still bound by the earlier restraints placed on their attitudes and behaviors. Just like the elephants, they will assume they are still fully bound and tethered by the negative treatment they received earlier.

Are restraints holding your people back? How tightly are you holding the leash? There may be something that you are unaware of in your leadership style or the company culture that is restraining the tremendous force and energy your employees are capable of putting to use.

For example, it's good to have a positive attitude about things, but if you create an atmosphere of "Don't say anything negative around here," then guess what! They will become trained, and pretty soon all you'll hear is good news. You'll be insulated from the bad news, and blind to what's really going on.

Don't tie your people down with chains, or even ribbons. The competition may fleece you while your people are telling you how great things are going.

Application

Ask yourself:

1 Do you have any personal behaviors or preferences that may be restricting your people's creativity and expression?

2 Are there any parts of your organization's culture that might be conditioning your people to hold back, such as fear of failure or excessive focus on good news, policies, or schedules?

3 What specific things do you do to reward open communication and innovation?

4 Are there any ways in which your management style is unintentionally limiting your team's thinking?

If we chain our people down, they become conditioned to the restraint, and soon, their innovation dies.

Lesson 8
Two Friends and a Giant

Related Leadership Dimensions
Team Building
Ego Management
Valuing Others
Organizational Savvy

EQUOIA TREES stand tall and firm. For 3,000 years they have been growing. There is no organism larger on the earth than these massive trees we call giants.

It would seem likely that being of such grand stature, the sequoia could continue on its own without any outside help. It looms taller and bigger than anything else in its world and seems to be self-contained in its power, but such is not the case. Without two little friends, our giant would cease to exist.

The first friend is the chickaree squirrel. Its favorite food is the tender green pine cone that grows on the sequoia tree.

The small squirrel voraciously eats the fresh, green scales of the young cones, and in the process, releases seeds entombed inside the cones. Following an instinctive urge to store, the chickaree also hides many cones for the future in wet, cool places beneath nearby fallen trees. When the chickaree returns to eat its stash in the fall and winter, it scatters many seeds as it eats. After being stored in the cool earth all winter, the seeds are ready for germination as spring approaches.

The giant's second friend is a wood-boring beetle. It uses the sequoia's cones as a nest for laying its eggs. When the eggs hatch, the larvae feed on the scales of the cones. By burrowing inside the cone they cut off the water supply and the cone dries up and dies. This causes the scales to turn brown and separate, which releases the seeds.

Together, the chickaree squirrel and the beetle help the giant continue to live and prosper. The mighty tree cannot release its cones alone. To survive, it must rely on its tiny friends to spread the next generation into the soil.

Through nature's planned teamwork and cooperation with the giant, the chickaree and the beetle provide a nurturing atmosphere that ensures the prosperity of all. The beetle and chickaree receive food and shelter. In exchange, they help the sequoia reproduce. Without the giant bending to take help from its little friends, its greatness would die out.

So it is in the human world. Some feel invincible, extremely self-reliant, and all-powerful. They never imagine that they need help from those they view as "below" them. But they are wrong. We cannot make it alone. It doesn't matter how big we are. As soon as we are too tall to let a small one help us, we are doomed to extinction.

Application

Ask yourself:

1 Do you feel self-reliant to the point that you need little help in your achievements? If you feel this way, think again.

2 Consider the many others you rely on to accomplish your tasks and meet your goals. Do you acknowledge and recognize the contributions of others?

3 What do you provide them in return?

As soon as you are too tall to let a small one help you, you are doomed to extinction.

Lesson 9
Processionary Caterpillars

Related Leadership Dimensions
Innovation
Focusing on Results
Inspiring Commitment
Team Building

ROCESSIONARY CATERPILLARS eat pine needles. They move through the trees like a little train, one leading and the others following, each with its eyes half closed and its head snugly fitted against the rear end of the one in front.

Scientists have placed groups of these caterpillars into continuous lines with the first one connected to the last, forming a complete circle with no gaps.

Around and around they go. They do eventually figure out that they are not getting anywhere. But it takes them several hours (sometimes ten or more) to break their circular, unproductive crawling.

Like these caterpillars, we sometimes feel bound to follow custom, precedent, tradition, habit, standard practice, company policy, or whatever you choose to call it. When we adhere so tightly to any of these things—without stopping to consider if there is a better way—we often waste precious time going in circles.

Are there any processionary caterpillars in your team? Are your people's eyes half closed? Do they methodically follow the person ahead of them? Do they, without question, blindly perform their tasks "the way it has always been done," with no thought of improvement or change?

Take a critical look at your rules, policies, and procedures—however well-intentioned, effective, or efficient they may seem. Do they become straitjackets and blinders on your people? Or does their work environment allow them to question the old ways without fear of retaliation?

Take a minute to ask, "Why are we doing this?" and encourage your people to do the same. Avoid the tendency to answer, "That's the way we do things around here."

Avoid mistaking activity for accomplishment. Don't become a processionary caterpillar.

Question the status quo. Work smarter, not harder!

Application

A few tips:

1 From time to time, (diplomatically) ask why certain policies or directions are being taken.

2 You may often learn that department or company regulations or procedures are the result of circumstances that

are now outdated and should be questioned and possibly revised.

3 Look for energy and resources that support mere busyness. How could they be channeled toward greater accomplishment?

Don't become processionary. Question the status quo. Work smarter, not harder!

Lesson 10
A Twenty-Cent Light Bulb

Related Leadership Dimensions
Problem Solving
Focusing on Results
Change Management
Strategic Thinking
Customer Focus

IN DECEMBER 1972, a Lockheed L-1011 jumbo jet left New York's John F. Kennedy International Airport bound for Miami, Florida. The late-night flight was uneventful until the jet began its initial descent into Miami International Airport. The pilots lowered the landing gear, then noticed that one light on their control panel did not illuminate.

This particular light indicated whether or not the nose landing gear had successfully lowered and locked into position. The pilots dared not attempt landing the plane without successful deployment of the nose wheel. The pilots radioed the tower and explained the situation. The tower approved their plan to return to a 2,000-foot elevation and maintain a circling holding pattern over the dark Everglades while the crew attempted to solve the landing gear problem.

While the crew worked on resolving what seemed to be the only issue they faced, a far more serious problem developed and went unnoticed: the plane's autopilot system was inadvertently disengaged and the plane began a gradual descent toward the dark swamp below. The plane's systems warned the crew that their altitude was decreasing, but the pilots and engineers were so intently focused on addressing the problem of the light bulb and landing gear, they failed to hear the warning chime that could have prevented the crash.

Too late, the pilots finally noticed that the plane had lost altitude. It crashed into the Everglades and over one hundred passengers and crew lost their lives. In the investigation that took place following the crash, it was determined that the nose landing gear was in perfect working order and had fully extended. The only thing not working was a small, inexpensive green light bulb in the control panel that had burned out.

The crew was so preoccupied, they ignored the remainder of the plane's systems—even critical alarm signals. A tragedy could have been avoided if they had focused their attention on the whole system, rather than on a single part.

It is easy to become distracted and miss the real target. Do you face problems at work that sap your energy and block your perspective of the big picture? Don't become so focused on dealing with immediate issues that you fail to notice significant warning signs of larger problems. It is never worth the risk to ignore systems that are in place to protect your company, department, or a specific project.

The lesson of the light bulb suggests the need for checks and balances—ways to ensure that at least one person is monitoring each part of your "system." It teaches us to maintain a holistic view of our work, even while we tackle minute problems. It reminds us to always focus on the things that matter most.

Application

A few tips:

1 Make sure you have elements in place to monitor your "whole system" as well as the individual parts, so you know if you are on track.

2 Initiate safeguards to ensure that no element of your organization that is essential to your overall success is overlooked, even in a crisis.

3 Consider what accountability processes you could use to ensure that delegated tasks and small-group assignments are completed effectively within the larger context of your organization's goals.

Always focus on the things that matter most.

Lesson 11

A Spider in Space

A FEW YEARS AGO, a group of students won the opportunity to submit an experiment for a shuttle flight into space. As a result, the space shuttle carried a special passenger into orbit for the first time: a spider. The students wanted to see how well the spider could adapt to weightlessness in its new zero-gravity environment.

Think for a moment of what spiders do best—spin webs. These webs are often extremely intricate. The process of spinning a web is an amazing feat of nature. Using its own weight, the spider first spins crosslines that serve as a frame for the sticky, spiral threads that later complete the web. But this natural process changed in an instant when our eight-legged astronaut was confronted with a shocking alteration in her environment for which nature had never prepared her. As she attempted to spin her web in space, she discovered there was no gravity to pull her from point A to point B. Every rule and condition of her previous existence had dramatically and completely changed. Her web was a total failure.

However, she did not give up. After many failed attempts, and considerable trial and error, she figured out that she could actually "swim" through the air like a water strider bug on the surface of a pool. Using this technique, the adaptable little spider soon completed a web. Through patient persistence, she mastered her web-making skills in a totally new environment, even though all she had previously known was so different.

Sometimes we experience surprising, unanticipated changes in our environment. There is a major upheaval, and suddenly, the rules change. The rug is pulled out from under us. If we are to survive, we have no choice but to figure out new ways of achieving our intended results.

Adapting to change is seldom easy, nor is it comfortable, but it is absolutely essential for survival. Let's take heart from our little hero. If a spider can figure out how to spin a web in zero gravity, surely we can manage the sometimes astronomical challenges thrown at us.

Application

Ask yourself:

1 Consider major changes you have experienced. How did you react to them? What skills did you adapt? What new talents did you develop to survive? In the end, did you find you could adapt to new rules, new surroundings, and new people?

2 When faced with dramatic shifts in your usual environment, calmly assess your situation. How can you modify or recalibrate your tools or approach?

3 Adaptability and flexibility are keys to succeeding in an ever-changing world. What skills would make you more adaptive?

If we are to survive, we have no choice but to figure out new ways of achieving our intended results.

Lesson 12
A Piece of Cake

ONE DAY, a professor brought a beautifully decorated cake to her class. She presented it on a table in front of the class for all to admire and to tantalize their taste buds. She then asked a pupil in the front row if he would like a piece of the cake. The pupil excitedly exclaimed, "Of course!"

The professor nodded, carefully took out a plate, set it next to the cake, and paused as she beheld this decadent confectionary creation. Then, in a sudden motion, she grabbed a handful of cake, plopped it on the plate, and shoved it into the student's lap. Smiling, the professor said, "Bon appétit." The student sat in shock staring at the blob of cake and frosting in his lap.

The professor explained that often, the hard work we put into our projects, assignments, or tasks can be marred by our presentation. The student had received the cake, but it was given in a way that prevented him from truly appreciating and enjoying it. The task was completed, but the quality of the content was diminished or lost by the presentation.

In contrast, Airbnb, a company that now offers more lodging listings than any hospitality chain in the world, realizes and uses the power of effective presentation. They initiated a policy early on that set them apart from other room-listing sites by offering, at no charge, a professional photographer to shoot photographs for the host's Airbnb profile. This gave them a clean, respectable, and safe presentation, which has translated into millions of successful transactions. They found that blurry and dark owner photos had decreased sales. The "cake" was much more desirable when cut beautifully and professionally, and presented cleanly on a plate.

We often spend hours, days, weeks, or even months, on the makeup of professional tasks and projects. Unfortunately, these can turn out underappreciated or misunderstood when a similar level of effort and forethought is not also given to how they are presented. This can also be applied to how we present ourselves as industry leaders to our bosses, colleagues, customers, and competitors. Remember, how we deliver the information is often just as important as the information itself. Your professional efforts can have good content, yet will likely be overlooked, misunderstood, or avoided, if not presented in an appealing manner, just like a piece of cake.

Application

Ask yourself:

1 Do you take the time to consider how best to present information to maximize its appeal, understanding, and benefit?

2 How do you present yourself each day in a professional set-
   ting? Consider your appearance, language, and gestures.
   Do these match your career aspirations?

3 Like any good skill, the best way to improve is to practice,
   practice, practice.

4 Are you actively seeking feedback on how you are perceived
   in professional settings, particularly as you communicate
   and share information with others?

5 Do you customize your presentation to the needs and inter-
   ests of the audience?

**How we deliver information is often just as important as the infor-
mation itself.**

Lesson 13
The Thick and Thin of It

Related Leadership Dimensions
Innovation
Problem Solving
Customer Focus
Focusing on Results

IT HAD BEEN a long, hard day for the workers at Moon's Lake House in Saratoga Springs, New York. It was the peak of the season and the rich and famous were out in abundance. For them, the evening was an unrestricted time of relaxation and pleasure. For the hotel workers, it meant long, hard hours of work trying to please their guests.

George Crum was the chef of the elegant dining room. He was required to treat every customer with dignity and present them with fine food. The demands on him were plentiful as he persisted in maintaining the high standards required by the patrons.

One evening, a particularly fussy patron had come to dine. The usual, thick-cut french fries did not please him. He rejected the order. So Chef Crum cut a thinner batch, fried them, and sent them out. These too were rejected by the patron with the same complaint that the fries were too thick. At this point, George decided to teach the patron a lesson. He sliced a potato as thin as he could, fried the pieces in lard and sent these thin—so thin they could never be pierced with a fork—french fries to the bothersome patron. But George's plan backfired. The patron wasn't upset, he was delighted! And other patrons soon wanted their own orders of these thin, fried potatoes.

From the thick comes the thin: in this case, the Saratoga Chip, as it was first called. To us, it is the well-known potato chip. It would become the most popular snack food in America. And don't forget all of the copycat and offshoot products that are flooding the chip and snack food market today—resulting in tens of billions in annual sales.

That demanding and ornery customer didn't look like an opportunity on that long and tiring night. That's the trouble with opportunities—they often come in disguises, such as disappointments, challenges, demands, failures, and frustrations. When we look long enough, dig deep enough, and work hard enough, the opportunity—and success—emerges from disguise.

Application

A few tips:

1 When you find yourself struggling under intense pressure due to an unforeseen shortage, brainstorm alternative solutions. You may be pleasantly surprised with the result!

2 View major challenges or setbacks as opportunities for innovation and creativity.

3 Customer demands may appear unreasonable but may, in the end, be a disguised blessing.

Opportunities often come in unpleasant disguises that must be removed with effort and ingenuity.

Lesson 14
Links in a Chain

Related Leadership Dimensions
Innovation
Personal Development
Focusing on Results
Change Management

IN AN ORDINARY but somewhat messy London laboratory, a world-changing discovery was accidentally made.
Dr. Alexander Fleming was investigating the properties of
Staphylococcus bacteria. He stacked his cultures of the bacteria in the lab, left on holiday with his family, and returned to
find mold growing in one culture. Curiously, the mold was killing the bacteria around it. Looking back, Dr. Fleming said, "I
certainly didn't plan to revolutionize all medicine by discovering the world's first antibiotic . . . but I suppose that was exactly
what I did."

There was a long road from discovery to a revolutionized world of medicine, however. Fleming grew the mold in a pure culture and isolated the substance that actually killed disease-causing bacteria. He published his findings, but the article received little attention. He continued to investigate the possibilities, but growing the mold, which Fleming named penicillin, was quite difficult. Isolating the antibiotic agent was even more difficult; its action on bacteria in cultures appeared to be fairly slow. Fleming felt that, because of the difficulty of producing it in quantity, and because of its slow impact, penicillin would never be important in treating infection—it just didn't seem effective enough to make a difference. He was also convinced that penicillin wouldn't last long enough in the human body. Some clinical tests showed promise, but most were inconclusive.

Fleming tried for years to find a chemist with enough skill to refine usable penicillin to enable further testing and mass production. He was never able to recruit a chemist, so he abandoned penicillin.

At about that time, Ernst Chain, a biochemist, and Howard Florey, a pharmacologist and pathologist, began researching and mass-producing penicillin using funds from the US and British governments (motivated to find a way to treat wounded Allied soldiers during World War II so as to avoid life-threatening bacterial infections). When D-Day came, penicillin was ready.

The Nobel Committee honored these three men with a Nobel Prize in Medicine. But they were not alone, as many others contributed as well. It took many years, persistent work, and multiple strands of research, financial support, and trial and error to turn an accidental discovery into a life-saving miracle drug.

As with penicillin, our best accomplishments are usually the result of slow growth and continuous effort. Consider the support and input from others who have helped you achieve your goals. Look at potential teaming relationships that will build on shared talents. Your persistent work may not change the entire world, but it will change yours.

Application

Think of the challenges you have faced recently, and all the tedious time you have spent on them.

1 When was a time that you experienced frustration or a major setback?

2 It is reassuring to note that the greatest minds in history had the same feelings. They just kept at it and learned from each setback. What do you do to build your personal resilience when you experience successive challenges or failures?

3 Persistence and patience are key elements in most success. How have you seen others avoid getting pulled down and giving up?

Accidental discoveries don't generally change the world without hard work and persistence.

Lesson 15
Writing the Right Code

Related Leadership Dimensions
Inspiring Commitment
Personal Integrity
Team Building
Valuing Others
Decision Making

W E TEND to think of the challenges of managing a virtual or nontraditional work team as a rather recent phenomenon made possible by advances in internet and communication technology. But more than fifty years ago, British entrepreneur Dame Stephanie Shirley built a successful software company that employed and inspired thousands of people, most of whom worked from home.

From Shirley's autobiography, *Let It Go*, we learn her success is even more remarkable in light of the fact that she escaped from Nazi Germany at the age of five as a Kinder-transport child sent to England. In school, she showed a real aptitude and interest for math, but ran into significant road-blocks because of gender bias in postwar Britain. In fact, she had to obtain special permission to receive instruction in mathematics from an adjacent boys' school because it was not offered at her all-girls school.

Early in her career, she worked at the British Post Office Research Station building computers from scratch and then writing machine code to operate them. Finally, striking out on her own, Shirley founded a small software company. Free-lance Programmers was created with start-up capital of only six pounds. Undaunted, she successfully recruited and trained a workforce of talented stay-at-home mothers who had few other choices for employment at the time. These employees were excited to make a difference in technology, expand their role as women, and support their families at home.

Shirley pioneered how she connected her employees and motivated them to achieve more than what society approved at that time by using flexible work methods, job sharing, profit sharing, and employee ownership. She adopted a "Trust the Staff" philosophy to allow each employee to feel valued. To manage projects, she used flow charts to define the tasks to be done and implement respective timelines. Communi-cation was primarily conducted through the use of a simple telephone.

This was all accomplished at a time when Shirley aggres-sively fought the battles for equal work and equal pay for women. She couldn't even open a bank account without her husband's permission. She changed her name to "Steve" in her business correspondence in order to be viewed as a legit-imate business person.

Now Dame Stephanie Shirley is a wealthy philanthropist and true inspiration for her team and other women in business. When asked why she gives away so much of her time and money, she humbly replies, "I do it because of my personal history; I need to justify the fact that my life was saved so many years ago."

Dame Shirley knew the importance of providing for the unique needs of her team members to inspire commitment. It is because of her pioneering spirit and her ability to unite her people around a common goal that she successfully built one of the first women-led technology companies. She understood that when you make decisions without creative input from the appropriate people, they may respond with outward acceptance, but never fully commit to supporting the decision or policy. Conversely, when you include your people in decision-making, shaping policies, and adopting programs, you demonstrate that you value them. When you recognize achievements, you reinforce your commitment to your people's success. When they see how you demonstrate your commitment to them, the team rewards you with increased effort, trust, and support. It is with this formula that Dame Stephanie Shirley truly learned how to write the right code to engage her people.

Application

Here are a few points for reflection:

1 How do you demonstrate your commitment to others? Are you focused on increasing the engagement of your team?

2 Are you resilient following setbacks? Do you actively seek the input of others, particularly your team, in decision making?

3 Do you actively seek ways to "give back"?

4 Are there untapped markets of opportunity (potentially within your organization) that call for you to inspire, empower, and champion?

5 Do you question or challenge the status quo? Are traditional procedures and practices still the most effective or appropriate?

When you demonstrate your commitment to your team, they reward you with increased effort, trust, and support.

Lesson 16
The Decision That Changed the World

Related Leadership Dimensions
Strategic Thinking
Decision Making
Innovation
Customer Focus
Delegating
Presentation Skills

I**T WAS** January 9, 2007, and Steve Jobs gave one of the most incredible presentations of both his life and in the history of consumer electronics. He said he would be introducing a wide-screen iPod, a revolutionary new mobile phone, and a breakthrough internet device that could be controlled with one simple stylus . . . the human finger. But it wasn't three products. It was just one product: the iPhone.

Jobs then demonstrated that this new "smart" device had a multitouch interface that let iPhone users smoothly pinch to zoom, employ physics-based interactivity that included inertial scrolling and rubber banding, and finally multitask to move seamlessly from listening to music to making a call, web surfing, or sending email, and back.

Almost overnight, a market that had been dominated by international cell phone manufacturers became obsolete. A revolutionary new paradigm of communication, digital interfacing, and portability was established, causing everyone else to play catch-up.

Apple could have focused on myriad other ventures, but they chose to focus their efforts on one large bet: the iPhone. This decision started at the top with Steve Jobs and cascaded down through the organization, aligning everyone with this new focus. Legions of teams planned, designed, decided, and executed on all of the necessary hardware and software elements to make the iPhone one of the most successful product releases in the history of technology.

Leadership is often distilled to prioritizing—deciding what to stop doing to focus on what you need to do. A leader must analyze opportunities, problems, and challenges from a big-picture perspective. Anticipate and plan for any and all variables. Focus tactics and team energies on key actions that will maximize and sustain organization position in the marketplace. This is the essence of strategic leadership.

Effective strategic practitioners always remember the big picture. They look for new discoveries and improvements every day. They create and deploy short- and long-term strategic and tactical plans to attain prioritized goals and objectives, measuring progress and outcomes along the way. For Apple, success in their new venture started with the clarity of an informed decision by a committed leader—a decision that ended up changing the world!

Application

Here are a few points for reflection:

1 In your daily work, do you prioritize some of your decisions? Or do you see them all as equal?

2 How do you stay informed on current and future market trends? Is this activity prioritized in your schedule?

3 Are you willing to make the effort to ensure that constant, clear communication occurs to align all individuals with the specified goal?

4 What metrics and reporting practices do you utilize to monitor progress toward identified goals?

5 Are the people who will be most impacted by the decision involved in making it? While seeking the opinions, insights, and perspectives of others, make sure you allow them to share freely before they know anything about your position in the matter.

Leadership is often distilled to prioritizing—deciding what to stop doing to focus on what you need to do.

Lesson 17
Big Ears Are a Must

HAVE YOU ever considered the remarkably disproportion-
ate body of a bat? It is quite small in comparison to the
size of its ears. But this isn't a trick of fate or DNA gone
haywire. There is a distinct purpose for this imbalance.

Bats live and hunt nocturnally. The night darkness per-
vades and distorts vision. If bats used only their eyes, they
would be incapable of successfully finding food or protecting
themselves against predators. So nature provided the help
they need.

Bats navigate their way through the darkness by the use of their own form of radar called *echolocation*. By making high-pitched squeaking noises, up to fifty per second, they create a barrage of sound waves. The waves bounce off objects in the path of the bat, giving it a remarkably accurate picture of the world around it. Using its extra-large ears, the bat picks up the echo and uses that information to determine its course of flight. It is thereby able to fly safely and successfully in the dark and obtain its food with great accuracy and efficiency.

The size of the ears is the fascinating point. They are huge in proportion to the rest of its small, mouselike body. Bats have learned to listen and receive feedback at a remarkably sophisticated level. Bats listen *actively*, not passively. If bats listened to the echoes of their squeaking as passively as many of us listen to each other, they would not last very long.

What would it be like if we concentrated on receiving feedback instead of giving it? That is, what if we spent more time listening with our ears than speaking with our mouths? The bat has taken an environment of darkness, and through developing excellent active listening skills, has prospered in that world, despite its challenges. Darkness becomes light because the bat is willing to listen and process what it hears. Let's take the time to develop some "bat radar" and start listening to the vital information that surrounds us.

Application

Here are some points for reflection.

1 The bat's two assets are listening and receiving feedback. How do you assess yourself in those two areas?

2 Can you see how helpful those skills are in "navigating" all types of situations and relationships?

3 Consider methods you can adopt that would improve your ability to listen effectively. Doing so will then increase the feedback you receive from those who know you and work with you.

How big are your ears?

Lesson 18
The No-Brain Stage

Related Leadership Dimensions
Valuing Others
Team Building
Coaching
Personal Development

TWO-YEAR-OLD CHILDREN. Ugh! That's the age the pediatricians refer to as the no-brain stage. The terrible twos, right? At this age, kids eat plants, rip up the newspaper, throw tantrums in the most public of places, pull off the tablecloth, get into everything, and test Mom's or Dad's patience to the limit. Many parents wish they could just park them somewhere. Then pick them up again when they have outgrown this age.

Think for a moment about the basic needs of two-year-old children. They need to be cared for. They need security and protection. They need to be listened to and included. They need their questions answered. They need love, reassurance, entertainment, attention, praise, and discipline. They need age-appropriate responsibilities.

We have just described the needs of two-year-olds. Think about it. Aren't these also the needs of a twenty-two-year-old, a forty-two-year-old, or a sixty-two-year-old—just a bit more sophisticated and complex? Read the previous paragraph one more time. The needs are similar. When you consider our basic needs, don't we all still have a two-year-old inside our grown bodies?

Do the people you lead sometimes seem like two-year-olds? They may whine, complain, and demonstrate selfish behavior. Do they ignore your requests, chronically procrastinate, waste time, or violate policies? If so, you may reach the point at which you want to just put them somewhere until they've grown up.

If that's the case, it may be because you're not filling their basic needs. Do you really care about them? Do you give them a feeling of security? Do you help them feel needed? Do you protect them from the powers that be? Do you genuinely listen to their concerns? Do you include them in decisions? Do you give them reassurance, attention, praise, and appropriate discipline? All of these questions reflect basic human needs—for two-year-olds or forty-two-year-olds.

If you're having trouble with your people, consider which of their "two-year-old" needs are not being met. This does not mean that you should treat them like two-year-olds. But if you satisfy their basic needs, they are much more likely to meet yours.

Application

Here are some points for reflection.

1 Consider the list of basic needs described in this story. Consider how people of all ages exhibit these needs.

2 When these needs are being met, people will be more productive. The opposite is also true.

3 Think of low-performance employees you struggle with. Then take a moment and analyze which of their needs are not being met. Are you able to fill the void?

If your people are acting like two-year-olds, ask yourself which of their "two-year-old needs" you may have neglected.

Lesson 19
True Blue Herons

Related Leadership Dimensions
Valuing Others
Team Building
Coaching
Personal Development

THE WATER spreads out in vast streams and inlets as it covers the swamplands. Many call this place home. Hidden on an island in the middle of the swamp are two birds that have made their nest at the top of a pepper tree.

These birds are great blue herons. With their tall legs, they can be spotted above the marshes standing still as statues. They are a beautiful and majestic sight.

Usually blue herons do not fly in large flocks, but prefer to remain in smaller groups. Only when it comes time for nesting do they gather together and create heronries far away and hidden from view. It is at this time that they pair off and form a cooperative working team that is remarkable.

Unlike most species, the male and female blue herons work together to build the nest. One will gather sticks and the other will weave them into a future home. After the large sticks are used to form a flat base, both will gather moss, leaves, and grasses to line the nest. When they are sure it is ready, the female will lay the eggs and then both take turns keeping the eggs warm.

Even as the eggs hatch, both heron parents continue to care for the babies. At first they are too small to eat whole food, so each parent chews the food and then feeds it to the baby birds. This process continues until the young are about eight weeks old. As the young mature, the parents teach them to fly and catch fish. It is not until they leave the nest that the two adults end their partnership.

From the beginning, the herons work together as a team. Each heron is willing to do whatever task is necessary to promote the success of its nest and brood. There is no quibbling about whether some jobs are beneath them. Neither is concerned about image or reputation. They don't wait to find out what's in it for them.

The same applies to us. The best and most successful teams are those filled with individual "true blue" members who possess these commendable qualities—eagerness to complete the task with no concern about status or position and no complaining about perceived fairness or treatment.

When there is commitment and willingness to work, success is far more likely. As the blue herons are true to each other in following through with their part, so can we be as we follow their example and remain "true blue."

Application

Here are some points for consideration.

1 Think of the attitudes of your people regarding their work. Are they enthusiastic and cooperative? Or are they focused on their own needs and concerned about personal recognition and prominence?

2 Now think of your own attitude. Are you modeling "true blue" qualities for your team to follow?

3 What can you change in your personal attitude and behavior to foster greater cooperation and enthusiasm among your team members?

4 What can you change in the culture of your organization to encourage "true blue" qualities?

When there is commitment and willingness to work, success is far more likely.

Lesson 20
The Farmer and the Rock

THERE WAS an old farmer who, year after year, had plowed around a large and expansive rock, as had his father before him. To the farmer, the rock was a source of constant irritation. He had broken several plow blades on it. He had to plant his crop rows on an angle around it—causing him to lose valuable space. Every year, he cursed the rock, but did his best to work around it.

Finally, one fall day, after having broken yet another plow blade on the rock, his anger provoked him to action. He took his tractor, a large chain, and a pick and shovel out to the field. He anticipated a long and difficult day's work. However, once he had swung his pick under the rock, he was amazed to discover that it was only a few inches thick. To his astonishment he was able to break up his old nemesis and remove the broken pieces with relative ease.

As he was hauling the broken pieces of rock away, he remembered all the trouble it had caused him and his father before him for decades. How he lamented the years of needless frustration because he had not chosen to confront the rock sooner.

Like the old farmer, do you ever "plow" *around* annoyances and obstacles in your path? Have you convinced yourself that removal of a problem is impossible—saying, "It's just too big to deal with"? We further aid our procrastination by telling ourselves we are "too busy to face it now." We may even deceive ourselves and say, "I'll come back to it later." Sometimes we rationalize, "It's not really my problem," and we blame someone else—excusing ourselves from being part of the solution. We may even accept having this chronic problem to the point that it actually brings a strange air of comfort due to familiarity—we are used to it. This is indeed a sad state.

When confronted with an obstacle, we are usually better off to gird up our determination, commit the time to confront the problem, and be done with it once and for all, as the farmer learned from his experience. The best way out of a problem is through it. And you are likely to discover that your cursed nemesis was actually much easier to resolve than you had imagined.

Application

Do the following:

1 List some of your annoyances that seem to always be there, especially those that really get in your way.

2 Is it time to stop "plowing" around them and confront them head on?

3 You may be surprised by the progress you make in "breaking up" your obstacles. They may be much easier to haul out of your life than you imagined.

The best way out of a problem is through it.

Lesson 21

It's Only Two Degrees

Related Leadership Dimensions
Personal Integrity
Dependability
Focusing on Results
Personal Development
Strategic Thinking

WHAT STARTED as a fun, adventurous sightseeing trip to Antarctica ended in a tragedy that killed every person on board the plane. Unbeknownst to the pilots, someone had modified the flight coordinates by only two degrees—a small difference with huge ramifications. This seemingly insignificant error placed the airplane twenty-eight miles east of where they should have been—and where the pilots assumed they were. As the aircraft approached Antarctica, the pilots decreased altitude in order to give the passengers a better view of the pristine, breathtaking landscape.

Neither of the pilots had made this particular flight before, but both were very experienced and expected no difficulties. There was no way they could have known that the error, a change of just two degrees, had placed them in the path of the active volcano Mount Erebus, which rises 12,000 feet from the frozen ground.

The plane flew on. The white of the snow that covered the volcano blended into the white of the clouds above and behind it. All this white made it appear as if they were flying over flat ground. By the time the instruments warned the pilots that the ground was rapidly rising toward them, it was too late for them to correct the problem. The plane crashed into the volcano, killing all 257 passengers on impact.

Sometimes small errors seem harmless and we do not feel the need to correct them. Occasionally, we consciously choose to cut corners and make small concessions on matters that seem inconsequential at the time. The error or change often appears so small that it seems to be of little or no importance. We may think no one will notice. Or we think, if they do notice, they won't mind. Usually we believe that these small corner-cutting choices will make little difference in the end.

This is simply not true. Disastrous consequences can result from even very small errors or a deviation from what we know is best. If leaders are aware of errors or deviations, then they should be corrected. If course corrections cannot be made, then contingency plans can be initiated.

Whatever the circumstances, staying true to the charted course and maintaining accurate awareness of where you are headed is the best way to ensure success. This applies to an organization's direction as well as an individual's code of ethics and values. Even a minor deviation—a few degrees—may jeopardize the desired outcome.

Application

Here are some points for consideration.

1 Think of the responsibilities you have. How do you monitor them to prevent misdirection of course?

2 Consider the consequences of inaccurate (even if only slightly off) feedback to the success of a mission.

3 Recall experiences where timely data was not provided. What was the result?

4 Course correction is only possible when quick, reliable, and accurate notice is provided and then quickly acknowledged and acted on.

Even a minor deviation—a few degrees—may jeopardize what you hope to accomplish.

Lesson 22

Can You See It?

THE STORY is told of a young blind boy sitting on a corner with a sign that read: "I am blind, please help." Next to him was a hat intended to hold coins from passersby. His collection was meager; few coins were in the hat. A man came upon the scene, pulled a few coins from his pocket, and placed them in the hat. Then he took the sign, turned it over, and wrote a new message on it. He replaced the sign with the new words facing those who passed.

Soon, the hat began to fill up with coins and bills. Many people were now freely giving their money to the blind boy.

Later in the day, the man returned to check on the boy. The blind boy asked him, "Were you the one who changed my sign this morning? What did you write?"

"I only wrote the truth. I said what you said, but in a different way." He had written: "Today is a beautiful day, and I cannot see it."

We often fall into the trap of thinking that it doesn't matter how we present a particular message. We may settle for the first idea that comes into our heads and never seek to improve it. This is especially true when we are making minor presentations that do not seem to have much impact on our jobs.

But whether we are presenting a report to the boss, making a sales pitch to investors or buyers, interviewing for a job, seeking a promotion, or providing a briefing, we are judged by the impression we make. Our audience will leave the room with a feeling and perception of our capabilities and potential—negative or positive.

Good coaching advice includes this counsel: "A poor presentation can damage a career. An excellent one will enhance it." What can you do to develop creativity and greater professionalism in your presentations? What difference would it make if you used more care in how you presented ideas? What skills do you need to develop in order to prepare and give more polished and engaging presentations?

How can you craft a phrase so it grabs your audience and drives your point home? How we say something may be even more important than what we say. Fair or not, image, reputation, and success are at stake.

Application

A few tips:

1 Once you gather your content for a presentation, carefully look at how you will present it—your phrases, examples, and illustrations.

2 Carefully consider who will be in the room. Direct your appeal and content to them. What are their pet peeves? What are their needs and concerns? Ask others for their opinions as you prepare. They may offer a fresh perspective.

3 A good rule of thumb is to practice your presentation *out loud* to yourself before you give it.

How we say something may be even more important than what we say.

Lesson 23
One Sniff at a Time

Related Leadership Dimensions
Team Building
Valuing Others
Coaching
Inspiring Commitment
Effective Communication

ELIBERATELY, THE DOG moves forward, sniffing through the bags, stopping and going as his nose directs. With trained care he stops before a large suitcase and sits next to it. Upon closer inspection, a small package of cocaine is found hidden inside a makeup case.

It is not by accident that the package is discovered. It is the result of careful, deliberate, and lengthy training. The dog is a graduate of a special school that provides training in the detection of drugs. Even if the drug is hidden in something that seems to completely overwhelm its smell, the dog will succeed if it can smell at least 10 percent of the drug. How is this possible?

Through careful screening, dogs are chosen for entrance to the school. To begin the training, a bag of illegal drugs is used in a game of catch—a dog's favorite activity. If the dog continues to play, the distance is slowly increased and the dog is rewarded with encouragement. Next, the dog waits while its trainer hides the drug. Using its nose, not its eyes, the dog learns to detect the drug's location. After about a month of successful retrieving, the dog will be challenged to find the drug hidden inside a suitcase.

There will be only one suitcase containing a hidden drug in the beginning. As the dog improves, more empty suitcases are added. As the dog succeeds, the task is made more difficult. After about two months, the dog is ready for the last test. The drug is hidden inside an item that has a potent smell. If the dog successfully finds that drug, it is ready for the real-world tasks of being an official drug detection dog.

Training of people is very similar. A good leader will never go faster than the success rate of the group. Clear instructions, realistic yet challenging goals, and positive reinforcement provide the best learning environment. If employees are supported and properly trained, if they work in an environment that is free of fear, and they feel positive about their growth, there will be an increased level of performance. In direct contrast is the leader who places tremendous pressure on a group and forces them to move at an unrealistic time rate, instilling an element of fear and manipulation into the people.

Drug dogs are specifically helped to understand exactly what is required of them, and they are given adequate preparation for the task. The trainer individualizes the training to each dog. The results are outstanding. Though we do not want to manipulate people like dogs and teach them to catch and fetch, we can learn to follow this simple plan: have the desired skill in mind, then slowly teach it through gradual approximations to the desired outcome. Select and train your people with care, and then care about your people.

Application

A few tips:

1 Think of how you attempt to develop and train your people. Is it gradual, realistic, and reasonable?

2 Consider the support you provide them as they face new and tougher assignments.

3 Not everyone in your group will respond the same way. Each team member deserves to be treated individually for maximum effectiveness and growth.

Select and train your people with care, and then care about your people.

Lesson 24
Curing Potatoes

Related Leadership Dimensions
Innovation
Problem Solving
Change Management
Strategic Thinking
Focusing on Results

N A restaurant kitchen in Des Plaines, Illinois, a very concerned cook offered a sample from a batch of freshly cooked french fries. He watched with dismay as the same worried frown crossed his boss's face. The staff had been cooking samples of french fries for many days now, but had not been able to please him. The cooks were trying to duplicate an exact taste and were not meeting with success. Something was very wrong and panic was beginning to creep into the picture. The restaurant was to open in just a few days. Without its number one menu item, how would it succeed?

A great deal of effort and energy had been expended up to this point. As with all dreams, there is a lot of sweat that is mixed into the success of a new endeavor. The boss had come so close and had surmounted so many obstacles, but now he seemed to have reached an impasse. Even a group from the Potato and Onion Association of the state could not figure out what was going wrong. He had one final hope. A scientist friend had offered to conduct some experiments and see if he could shed some light on the situation.

The experiments proved successful. It was a simple matter of environment. When the McDonald brothers stored their potatoes, they did so outside in chicken wire bins. The dry desert winds of San Bernardino, California, had a curing effect on the potatoes, giving them a special taste when cut and fried. Ray Kroc was in Illinois, trying to duplicate the same procedure. He had been storing his potatoes in a wet, cool basement. His potatoes had a mushy taste in contrast to the McDonald brothers' crisp taste. From then on, all potatoes were cured using large electric fans while in storage to simulate the desert air. It was a simple solution to what had at first appeared to be an impossible problem.

The transplanting of an idea is not a simple task. It takes meticulous and diligent devotion to minute detail to ensure its success. If the idea is not kept in a free-flowing current, unrestrained by doubt and skepticism, it will fail to grow. Just like the potatoes needing to be cured in a fresh-air environment, so does an idea. If it is stored in a dark and damp basement, it will be tasteless. Nurture and develop your ideas with light, energy, and encouragement. Your persistence will pay off!

Application

Here are some points for consideration.

1 Recall successful ideas that you have witnessed over the years. Notice how they usually required time and patience before they reached fruition.

2 These ideas often needed the influence of individuals who brought a new perspective and asked different questions.

3 In taking concepts, products, and practices to the next level, don't overlook small and seemingly insignificant details that often play a major role.

Are you giving new ideas enough fresh air?

Lesson 25
Big Bear, Little Ego

Related Leadership Dimensions
Team Building
Ego Management
Inspiring Commitment
Organizational Savvy
Focusing on Results

ONE OF the most successful and revered football coaches in the history of this American sport had a personal philosophy that is priceless. Coach Bear Bryant said: "I'm just a plow hand from Arkansas, but I have learned how to hold a team together. How to lift some men up, how to calm down others, until finally they've got one heartbeat together, a team. There are just three things I'd ever say: 'If anything goes bad, I did it. If anything goes semi-good, then we did it. If anything goes really good, then you did it.' That's all it takes to get people to win football games for you."

His philosophy paid off big in football: During his years coaching the University of Alabama football team, he amassed thirteen conference and six national championships. For several years, he held the record for the most wins as a head coach in collegiate football history. That's a remarkable record by any standard. But there's more to the story.

Young Bear Bryant started his collegiate football career before he had even finished high school—he was that good. But he understood the importance of the team, and knew that his individual efforts were important only in light of how they contributed to the success of the team. Bryant was one of two receivers on the Alabama team. Don Hutson, later inducted into the NFL Hall of Fame, who was a big Alabama star during his college years, was the other receiver. Bear humbly and humorously described himself as the "other end" and didn't worry about who got the credit or the newspaper write-ups.

When Pearl Harbor was bombed in 1941 and the US entered World War II, Coach Bryant walked away from coaching to join the United States Navy. When his ship was rammed and they were ordered to abandon ship, Coach Bryant ignored the order and saved the lives of his men—his team. This is a man who understood what it meant to be a team player. Even as the leader, he always saw himself as part of the team—and no better than the other parts.

Your team knows whether you, as the leader, really see yourself as one of them, with shared goals and shared burdens. What a difference it makes to give your team members your support, to be with them! When the heat is on, shield them from the powers above, and take the blame for their mistakes. When things are going well, give them recognition. That's how champions are made, on the field, in the home, and at work.

Application

A few tips:

1 As a leader, be careful not to consider yourself more important than your team. You merely have a different level of responsibility.

2 In good times, let the team receive the credit and glory. In tough times, shield them. They will sense your commitment to them.

3 Do all you can to help them succeed as a team. No one is more important than all of them.

"If anything goes bad, I did it. If anything goes semi-good, then we did it. If anything goes really good, then you did it. That's all it takes..."

Lesson 26
Blinded by an Egg

THE STORY is told that when Columbus returned from his historic voyage to the New World, the Spanish Court held a royal banquet in his honor. His accomplishments were formally honored by King Ferdinand and Queen Isabella, but apparently not everyone felt that he was worthy of special recognition. It was while sitting at this banquet that Columbus taught a great lesson.

It seems that those sitting close by did not think that it took much talent to discover anything, especially the New World.

123

They felt that anyone who set out in the correct direction would easily find it sooner or later. They could not see what all the fuss was about.

Rather than answer these insults, Columbus instead posed a problem. He requested that a whole fresh egg be brought to him, and asked if anyone could make it stand on its end. His skeptics tried many times but were unable to succeed. They told Columbus that it could not be done. Columbus took the egg and gently smashed the bottom against the table, crushing its tip, but leaving the rest of the shell intact. Then he removed his hand and the egg remained on the table standing comfortably on its end.

Once this solution was shown to them, it seemed obvious and easy. All were able to replicate the solution. But discovery has no example, no easy or obvious path to follow. Explorers must make their own way without the advantage of knowing the end from the beginning—that is what makes discovery so remarkable.

When a horse pulls a cart through a busy street, its owner often places blinders at the sides of its eyes so that it will not be distracted. Its peripheral vision is restricted so that the horse will see only what is straight in front of it. Blinders keep the horse and its cargo safe.

Maybe the royal experts—skeptics—at the banquet honoring Columbus preferred safety to discovery, because they chose mental blinders over the risk of seeking something new. Only after the discovery was no longer new could they see how to find it. Their blinders kept them from solving the egg riddle, and it kept them safely in Europe while others were discovering new worlds.

When Columbus ventured out to find a new path to the East, he did not restrict his vision with mental blinders. Be willing to remove established blinders and allow your vision to see all available options. Assess your level of risk aversion. Could you have solved the dilemma of the egg before the solution was given? View challenges in a new light. Real discoveries come only through a change of attitude and perspective.

Application

Here are some points for consideration.

1 Ponder the types of mental "blinders" you put on, thus restricting your view of the possibilities.

2 Celebrate with those who discover, and learn from how they did it.

3 Risk and discovery go hand in hand—you must deal with risk directly as you follow the path of discovery.

Discovery has no example, no easy path to follow. Are you willing to see and search out unknown routes?

Lesson 27
Trees That Are Hollow

Related Leadership Dimensions
Personal Integrity
Personal Development
Dependability
Decision Making
Inspiring Commitment

THERE IS nothing more picturesque than a tree-lined street. We love trees for their beauty and for what they provide—be it shade, fruit, syrup, or lumber. We also appreciate what they symbolize: strength, endurance, steady growth, and renewal.

On just such a tree-lined street stands a tree that looks like its fellows—tall, straight, sturdy, and beautiful. But come closer, look around the tree, and you will find that it is hollow. Something happened, long ago, that weakened the trunk.

Year after year, instead of steady growth, this tree experienced steady decay. Now it relies on steel reinforcements to stand straight and tall like the trees around it.

Because holes will be filled, the tree is full of all kinds of waste, making its hollowness even more profound. Instead of a strong trunk that carries nutrients to the branches, this tree has garbage enclosed in bark.

Just as trees grow slowly and steadily through the years when they have the proper nutrients and conditions, people's characters grow steadily from day to day and year to year. With the right choices, a person will grow into a strong, upright individual who is guided by an inner sense of right and wrong, and self-worth. People who grow this way will be honest, hardworking, and fair. They will be a force for good in the workplace and the community. Personal integrity will be more important to them than any other measure of success.

Unfortunately, it is also possible that negative, corrosive influences can weaken a person's growing character. Those who allow these influences to determine what they do will slowly decay. They may look and act (publicly, at least) just like every other person. But those who suffer from moral decay have lost their natural strength and goodness. They are hollow. The slow and steady loss of integrity leaves them empty and they will likely become receptacles of all types of waste.

Look inside—what do you find there? Emptiness and waste? Or strength, integrity, and honesty?

Application

A few tips:

1 Consider the choices you have made over the years. Are they consistent with your values?

2 Think of people you admire for their strength of character and code of ethics. How do you measure up to them?

3 Conduct a self-assessment to see ways you could be more consistent with the honesty and integrity you want to emulate.

Look inside. What do you find there? Emptiness and waste? Or strength of character, integrity, and honesty?

Lesson 28
The Dream Post

Related Leadership Dimensions
Personal Development
Focusing on Results
Personal Integrity
Coaching

ITH HIS illustrations tucked securely under his arm and with the confidence of a newly secured diploma, the nineteen-year-old entered the office. He carried a new business card that read: "Artist, Illustrator, Letterer, Cartoonist; sign painting, Christmas cards, calendars, magazine covers, frontispieces, still life, murals, portraits, layouts, design, etc."

This young man was willing to do just about anything that required a paintbrush! His wish from the time he was a small boy was to be an artist. In fact, he couldn't remember a time when he didn't want to be an artist. His calling card eventually got him inside the doors of the best publishing houses in the country.

Norman Rockwell's painting career lasted fifty-nine years, and he produced over four thousand paintings, including his most familiar work in the *Saturday Evening Post*. His artwork is recognized and loved by many. His paintings resonate with people far and wide. He painted recognizable scenes depicting common, everyday life: a happy gathering at a Thanksgiving feast, a soldier hugging family goodbye, a young couple sharing ice cream. His paintings adorned magazine covers, hung in offices, and decorated parlor walls. Yet, during his life and after, he was sharply criticized by fellow artists. They felt that his work was too simplistic and predictable. Some even refused to acknowledge him as an artist.

That never seemed to bother Rockwell. He painted what he loved. He painted, as his psychiatrist once told him, "his happiness." He stayed true to what he felt was important and ignored the critics.

In 1999, years after Rockwell's death, *New Yorker* art critic Peter Schjeldahl said, "Rockwell is terrific. It's become too tedious to pretend he isn't."

Sometimes we are tempted to seek approval from the few voices that are deemed expert. We may choose a path that will please the critics instead of the path that is a true reflection of our passions and abilities. In the end, our best comes when we are true to ourselves. If we want to excel, we must trust our passions, dreams, goals, and capacities. We must learn to shut out the voices of the world's "experts" and be true to who we are.

Application

A few tips:

1 Consider the career you are pursuing. Is it bringing you the happiness you dreamed of?

2 If not, analyze changes you could make that would incorporate your skills and talents in areas you truly enjoy.

3 As you pursue your dreams, don't give way to critics who enjoy tearing others down. Be true to yourself and your own happiness.

Our best success comes when we are true to ourselves.

Lesson 29
Color It Green

Related Leadership Dimensions
Team Building
Personal Development
Coaching
Innovation

SLUGGISHLY, THE LONG, dirty arms move along the branch of the giant tree. The form attached to the arms seems to be slumped like a glob of putty as it hangs suspended. It is hairy and stinky and ugly. On its belly are wiggly lines that appear to be moving.

The sloth is not out to win any race. In fact, it is one of the slowest mammals created. As it hangs upside down and slides its arms and legs along the branch, it has no other thought than to use the least amount of effort possible. It would rather be sleeping, which occupies most of its time. But it does have to eat, so it laboriously and begrudgingly performs this mundane task.

At first glance, the sloth has no redeeming qualities. It is filthy and antisocial. To add to its oddity, its hair grows from its tummy down towards its back. Because it is so dirty, green algae grows on its coat of hair. A pitiful creature, by all accounts.

But Mother Nature is kind. There is still a purpose to be found in the sloth. The green algae that forms so readily in the dirty hair actually serves a worthwhile purpose. The green color helps protect the sloth from enemies by providing a camouflage among the green leaves of the trees it calls home. The sloth, without knowing it, provides a good turn to another creature.

Remember those wiggly lines on its stomach? They are caterpillars. Moths love the cozy habitat of the sloths' green hair so they lay their eggs in it. The newly born caterpillars live off the algae until ready for their transformation into a moth.

We may all be tempted at times to view ourselves or our circumstances as pitiful and good for nothing. We seem, at times, to have eyes that see only the negative—in ourselves, in our peers, in our bosses, and in our circumstances. Look more closely. In the middle of a "green algae" person, you may see something worthwhile developing, despite the perception of an entirely negative appearance. During an unpleasant day that we have initially written off as a loss, we may change our view and see opportunities to explore or expand our strengths.

We can train ourselves to see and promote positive growth in less-than-ideal circumstances and people. If a sloth has that potential, then we certainly do. We can choose to cultivate the positive. We can look for opportunities that are buried in challenges. We can color ourselves, our people, or our circumstances any way we'd like.

Application

Here are a few points for consideration.

1 Ponder the way you judge others. Do you have a tendency to dismiss them because of appearance or mannerisms? Or because they are unusual?

2 As this happens, consider altering the filter through which you are viewing them. Consider seeing them in a different light.

3 You may be pleasantly surprised by the ways their uncommon characteristics can be matched with others to generate positive outcomes.

In the middle of a "green algae" person or day, you may see something good and useful developing.

Lesson 30
Dirty Laundry

Related Leadership Dimensions
Ego Management
Listening
Problem Solving
Valuing Others

THERE WAS an elderly couple who would sit together each morning for breakfast. The woman often looked out her kitchen window and saw her neighbor's laundry, which she'd hung out to dry, blowing in the wind. The woman frequently complained how dirty the laundry looked—how many brown spots were still on the clothes or that the whites were yellow and dingy. She grumbled to her husband that her neighbor was awful at doing laundry. This was a regular conversation for months, with increasing agitation, to the point at which the woman was ready to go over to her neighbor's house and instruct her on how to properly do laundry.

Then one day, while eating their morning meal, she was very surprised to observe her neighbor's laundry looking clean! There were no dirty spots and the whites were brilliant. The laundry blowing in the breeze appeared perfectly clean. She couldn't believe it. She looked at her husband and asked if he had told her neighbor to clean better. He said no. Exasperated, she wondered what had happened. Her husband finally told her that he had simply cleaned their kitchen windows.

This story illustrates how we often have blind spots that prevent us from seeing things clearly. As leaders, we may think we have the right answer, but perhaps we are viewing the world through a distorted or incorrect lens. We may not fully appreciate the biases or lenses through which we are viewing our own and others' behaviors. Rarely do we see things through a "clean window." We all have blind spots!

We've learned over the years that one of our biggest blind spots as leaders is developing relationships with others. We need to view these critical relationships accurately in order to build productive ones. In fact, effective leadership is grounded in effective relationships. The best way to become aware of our own blind spots is to actively solicit feedback from others. This will allow us to gain insight from a variety of perspectives. Take the elderly woman in the story: If she had gone outside and changed her perspective, she would have viewed her neighbor's laundry in a different light. She also might have been unwittingly ignoring previous comments from her husband or creating an environment in which he was not comfortable to share the honest truth with her about their dirty window. These can all occur within our own professional relationships. Let us actively seek different perspectives, discover our blind spots, and avoid viewing the world through a "dirty window."

Application

Here are a few points for reflection:

1 How do you learn about your personal blind spots? Do you take the time to consider them?

2 Examine each of your professional relationships—boss, direct reports, peers, and customers. Do you solicit feedback from them?

3 Do you listen to the input of others? Have you created an environment in which differing opinions can be freely shared?

4 Are you willing to admit when you don't know something or have a blind spot? It is in your best interest to examine your blind spots before assuming you know better than someone else.

Rarely do we see things through a "clean window." We all have blind spots!

Lesson 31
The Power of "Yes!"

Related Leadership Dimensions
Time Management
Personal Integrity
Decision Making
Valuing Others

THE ENTERTAINMENT industry is a demanding, fickle, and high-risk environment. Founded on intense creativity and marketing, it can be one of the most unlikely environments for long-term individual success. Yet out of this environment, we find a lesson that takes us "back home."

Shonda Rhimes, the media titan behind hit television shows *Grey's Anatomy*, *Private Practice*, and *Scandal*, was driven and always loved to work. However, in her biography she states that she eventually found herself "overworked, overused, overdone, and burned out." She asked herself,

"What do you do when the thing you do, the work you love, starts to taste like dust?" Her work depended on her amazing creative energy, but, almost overnight, POOF... it was gone! She continues, "I needed to figure out how to get my inspiration back! At almost the same time, I realized my family life was also in trouble." As a single parent, with these huge work commitments, she watched as her kids were quickly growing up and needed her attention more than ever.

Shonda made a critical decision. She notes, "I resolved to simply choose to always say yes to my kids first. I feared this would take an incredible amount of time, but have you noticed kids today have fairly short attention spans? These 'yes' requests only took about fifteen minutes before the kids were off onto something else, like homework, friends, or other commitments." The unexpected result was that by focusing on her kids, she slowly began to get her creative energy back. She discovered that the real source of what she calls her "buzz" came from the personal time she spent with her children.

At times, we can all relate to some of the feelings Shonda was experiencing. Work, projects, relationships, and life can all begin to feel less fulfilling. When you find that you are facing a life balance challenge, or even a crisis, try something new, something that you had been saying no to. Say yes and give it a try. As you do this, while obviously staying within your personal moral code, you may find that you benefit in several ways—ways that you've never imagined. Your life takes on a more desirable balance, and you have unleashed the power of "Yes!"

Application

Here are a few points for reflection:

1 What is the source of your "buzz?" What situations energize you physically and intellectually?

2 Do you place a high priority on these activities? How can you adjust your schedule accordingly?

3 Do you schedule personal time each day? This is particularly critical when you are feeling like your role is monotonous, or less than fulfilling. Are you taking on other people's responsibilities?

4 What is your method of prioritizing your demands? Do you identify what is most important and schedule them first?

5 Are you willing to "shake up" your routine? Try something different and see if you can get your creative juices flowing again. Look for new ways to bring needed balance to your life.

When facing a life balance challenge or even a crisis, try something new.

Lesson 32
Buying Hands and Feet

Related Leadership Dimensions
Inspiring Commitment
Valuing Others
Team Building
Listening
Personal Development

IT'S EASY for a company to buy a person's hands and feet, but what the organization really needs is its employees' hearts and heads.

You can buy a person's hands and feet for twenty or fifty dollars an hour, but that's all you will get—the person's hands and feet, and nothing else. That is a lose-lose situation for both the employer and the employee.

For these employees the best time of the week is Friday night. "Thank goodness it's Friday!" Right? They can't wait to get away from work and forget the place. Their most miserable time of the week is Sunday night. Why? Because they have to return to that hated place the next morning. Sound familiar? Of course it does. You've seen it play out often.

A "hands and feet" employee actively looks for opportunities to be absent from work. Given a choice between 1:30 or 4:30 for a dental appointment, he will choose 1:30—and then just let that stretch out through the rest of the afternoon. This is the kind of employee you may have to watch to make sure they are not surfing the Internet or playing computer games rather than doing their work. Lunch breaks tend to go over the allotted time, never under. And the quality of work from "hands and feet" employees is usually mediocre, at best.

How do you deal with these employees? Do you continuously try to manage hands and feet, or do you try to *earn* something more? How do you alter their attitude? How do you get genuine commitment out of your people? You must change the focus. It is your responsibility to earn their commitment. Treat them as you would want to be treated, and you'll get more than their hands and feet. Consider giving them more support, respect, and trust. Include them in decisions. Ask for their opinions. Listen to them. Help them feel valued. Then you will begin the process of earning their hearts and heads, along with the commitment and performance you're looking for. That is a win-win situation.

It is as Clarence Francis said: "You can buy a man's time, you can buy a man's physical presence at a given place, you can even buy a measured number of skilled muscular motions per hour or day. But you cannot buy enthusiasm . . . you cannot buy loyalty; you cannot buy the devotion of hearts, minds, and souls. You have to earn these things."

Application

A few tips:

1 Any organization can improve the level of commitment their employees have. How can you influence your organization?

2 Buying hands and feet is easy to do. It's the starting point. Identify your "hands and feet" employees. What can you do to earn their hearts and minds?

3 Earning the heart and mind is the real goal. This requires effort by the leader. It starts with viewing the employees as truly valued and respected. That is conveyed to the employees by the attitude and behavior of the leaders.

You cannot buy devotion, loyalty, trust, or commitment. You cannot buy hearts and minds—these can only be earned.

Lesson 33
Lobsters and Egos

Related Leadership Dimensions
Personal Development
Ego Management
Change Management
Organizational Savvy
Coaching

W HEN IT comes to receiving feedback about ourselves, most of us have shells as hard as a lobster. But that's not necessarily a bad thing.

Consider a lobster's life cycle and the role its shell plays. As it grows, the young lobster becomes too large for the shell that protects it. The lobster must then search for an area among the rocks on the ocean floor, where it can feel relatively secure from any predators. Slowly, it begins to shed the shell that is stunting its growth.

When the shell is gone, just consider its plight. Its new shell, which began growing before the old one was shed, is still soft and provides little protection. During this time, the lobster is extremely vulnerable and at great risk from predators. It is completely exposed to its dangerous world. Yet, the alternative would be worse. Without the periodic shedding of its shell, the lobster would not be able to grow.

Each of us has a protective shell. It's called our *ego*. Just like the lobster's shell, it protects us, but it can also prevent us from growing. Many of us, safe and secure inside our shells, are so worried about risk and vulnerability that we never grow. Because we are afraid of what we might find, we avoid all forms of feedback and constructive criticism about our own performance. We reject information about our work, our interactions with others, and our abilities and weaknesses. Ironically, when we hide so successfully from negative feedback, we also miss out on the positive feedback that accompanies it.

You have to periodically shed your protective ego and open yourself to feedback, both favorable and unfavorable, in order to grow. Like the lobster, it is healthy and progressive to find a safe place and voluntarily leave your old, worn-out shell. Yes, you will be vulnerable, and the process may hurt a bit, but your potential growth and improvement are well worth the risk.

Application

Ask yourself:

1 What is your honest attitude toward performance reviews and other opportunities to receive feedback?

2 Do you find you become defensive upon learning how you are perceived by your colleagues?

3 Are you open to feedback? The ego is vital to protecting us from all that life throws at us. It just needs to be managed. Feedback is very healthy—both good and bad—as it allows us to grow.

Find a safe place, step out of your shell, and open yourself to feedback—the growth is worth the risk.

Lesson 34
Navigating Like a Pigeon

Related Leadership Dimensions
Personal Development
Problem Solving
Change Management
Coaching
Ego Management

F YOU were transported one day by air to a secluded valley and left alone without a map or compass, would you be able to find your way home? For the average, untrained person this would be a very difficult task. For a pigeon it would be a piece of cake.

The homing pigeon has developed the ability to use multiple clues to help it find home. It is not dependent on just eyesight or smell. Nor is it luck or whimsical chance. By using every available element and all its senses, the homing pigeon consistently returns home.

Before beginning its journey, the pigeon notes the position of the sun or stars and orients itself to the direction of home. From tiny magnetic receptors located in its brain, it can read the earth's magnetic field and adjust its return flight accordingly. Through the detection of small changes in barometric pressure, a pigeon can detect a change of altitude and protect itself from natural barricades. Its sense of smell is on full alert to help it detect the homeward path as it flies. An ability to detect the direction of polarized light helps the pigeon verify its location. A final key is the pigeon's awareness of infrasound. These are very low sound waves, generated by such things as mountains, oceans, and storms, that can travel great distances. They provide a system of patterns the pigeon can follow. Eyesight appears to play only a minor role. In a field test, a group of pigeons whose vision was obscured by frosted glasses were still able to return home. It is this remarkable combination of multiple senses and clues that give the homing pigeon its well-deserved name.

The homing pigeon does not rely on just one or two of its skills to solve its problem of getting home. Instead it uses every available resource and, with that marvelous combination, is able to reach its goal and return home. By constantly staying aware and keeping its senses on full alert, it reaches its destination.

Too often, we rely on just one skill or one method of problem solving no matter what challenge we face. Limiting ourselves like this can leave additional skills and other solutions undeveloped, overlooked, or ignored. Over time, our strengths may actually cripple us because we fail to develop other available skills and methods for dealing with challenges, resolving issues, and overcoming crises.

Application

A few tips:

1 No doubt you are aware of some of your well-used strengths. You have lesser-used ones as well. Don't neglect these assets.

2 Observe how you have a tendency to rely on one or two dominant methods for solving a problem. That will limit your effectiveness. Experiment with other skills to augment your tool kit.

3 Become more adaptable and flexible in your leadership style. You will be better prepared for life's uncertainties by expanding your capabilities.

We need a fully developed skill set to successfully overcome the challenges that come our way.

Lesson 35
Follow the Bouncing Ball

Related Leadership Dimensions
Personal Development
Innovation
Change Management
Coaching
Inspiring Commitment

GIUSEPPE WAS the son of a fisherman. His father was the son of a fisherman. His father's father was the son of a fisherman—you get the idea. It was a family that had fished for its livelihood for many generations. The sea, with its rolling waves and salty breezes, was in their blood. Giuseppe's father was proud of the family's fishing heritage, and when he brought his family to America, he brought the tradition with them. He established himself on Fisherman's Wharf in San Francisco and expected Giuseppe to work by his side.

Giuseppe was proud of his heritage too. He diligently tried to follow the wishes of his father and the family tradition. He listened attentively and watched the fishermen. He tried to work alongside his father. But no matter how hard he tried, the boats made him seasick and the smell of fish didn't help.

What a disappointment Giuseppe was to his father. How could he be so prone to sickness and so ill-suited for a profession that had been in the family for generations? He wasn't too sick to play with his friends, so why was he letting his father down?

Giuseppe was unable to continue on the wharf, so he quit fishing and found work doing odd jobs in the town. He helped supply his family with extra money, but that didn't satisfy his father. He had broken tradition and that was unforgivable.

Luckily, Giuseppe discovered he had a rare talent. He applied the same diligent effort and attentive study to this talent as he had to learning to be a fisherman—but with far better results. Not only was he able to earn a living, but he also became quite famous for his skill. Perhaps he even made his dad proud. He certainly impressed others and was eventually idolized by millions. Giuseppe became a legend in his own time. You know him by his American name: Joe DiMaggio, the famous New York Yankees baseball player.

The situation Joe found himself in is quite common for anyone who has tried to break away from an expected traditional path. Striking out to try something new is a fearful challenge for many people. It takes great personal desire and determination. It is often met with endless skepticism and criticism. If Joe had remained a fisherman, not only would he have been sick and miserable, but more importantly, he would have missed developing something far greater in himself. Joe DiMaggio is an example of being able to look at your own life, take an inner desire, and with courage, follow it to success.

Application

Perhaps you broke the mold of family tradition in pursuing your own path. If so, you can relate to Joe. Do you feel confined to an expected path or are you able to break away and follow your dreams? Consider the following:

1 Part of your role as a leader is to coach others—to develop their abilities to grow and succeed. Help them discover opportunities that will provide them additional challenges and satisfaction.

2 Take advantage of aptitude assessments and professional feedback instruments for both you and your team members to identify potential skill areas and new competencies.

Your inner desires and talents can be the key to your success, if you follow them.

Lesson 36
Don't Be Ostrich Blind

A N OSTRICH is a remarkable bird. It can't fly, but it can do some pretty amazing things. Its long legs make it the fastest bird on land; it can run at speeds of up to forty-three miles per hour. It can maintain that speed for long distances, meaning that it can outrun even the speediest of predators.

It also has surprising strength. Its legs can deliver powerful kicks at its predators. Ostriches have been known to kill lions with a single, well-placed kick. Their eyes are two inches in diameter, considered the largest of any land vertebrate, which means that they can see predators from a great distance. They have three stomachs, so they can digest just about anything.

With all these strengths, it would seem that ostriches should be invulnerable to predators, and they generally are. But the ostrich has one weakness that can nullify all its strengths. It thinks that if it can't see you, you can't see it.

When trainers at an ostrich farm approach the ostrich, it reacts to them as if they are predators. It tries to run away, but since it is in an enclosed area, it doesn't get far. It kicks at them, but it can only kick forward, so the trainers easily avoid its kicks by approaching it from the rear. It pecks and tries to fight them off—until they slip a small hood over its head, covering its eyes. At that point, the ostrich becomes completely docile and allows the trainers to lead it wherever they want it to go. It no longer tries to fight them, not because it has changed its mind about their being predators, but because it believes it is invisible to them.

There are parallels to this form of blindness in our professional and personal lives. It is tempting to refuse to see potential risks in a given venture. It is all too easy to put unpleasant tasks out of our minds, hoping that they will somehow resolve themselves if we just ignore them for a while. And when "predators" are drawing closer, threatening our position, we may choose to discount or dismiss their advances and close our eyes to the threat they pose. But just because we choose not to acknowledge them does not make them disappear.

The good news is, like the ostrich, we usually already have the tools we need to overcome the challenges, risks, and threats to our success. We simply need to keep our eyes wide open and wisely use all our strengths and resources.

Application

In spite of all our skills and assets, like the ostrich, each of us usually has a blind spot that can be very dangerous if it remains unknown or ignored. Ask yourself:

1 Are you aware of your weaknesses? How did you learn about them? What do you do to protect yourself from them or compensate for them?

2 Do you ever hide from your weaknesses? Often a "cover your eyes" attitude will cause you to deny an eventuality or a likely pitfall.

Discuss this with a coach or trusted colleague to discover remedies to use when needed.

Closing your eyes to risks, challenges, and threats does not make them disappear. Keep your eyes wide open and face whatever comes.

Lesson 37
Saved by a Sneeze

Related Leadership Dimensions
Change Management
Innovation
Customer Focus
Strategic Thinking
Focusing on Results
Listening

WHEN A COLD hits and sneezing and sniffles ensue, what a comfort it is to know that you have your box of tissues close by your side, ready to rescue your suffering nose. Our noses would be lost without the comfort of "Kleenex."

In 1914, Kleenex was nowhere near your nose. At that time, it was performing a patriotic duty overseas, at the front lines. Called Cellucotton, it was used to dress the wounds of injured soldiers. An American company had responded to a War Department need by creating this new and remarkably soft cotton fabric, which performed its duty so well that it also served as an air filter for soldiers' gas masks.

After World War I ended, the company found itself the proud owner of warehouses of Cellucotton. Having been a bit too zealous, they had overproduced. Now they were stuck with something that was no longer needed, so Cellucotton was retired and given a civilian job.

Like all veterans, Cellucotton had to learn to adapt to a postwar world. It was given a new name, Kleenex Kerchiefs, and along with the help of beautiful models who advertised its use, began its new job. It was sold as a "sanitary cold cream remover" perfect for makeup removal. Women loved it. Kleenex Kerchiefs were a tremendous success and the bulging warehouses began to empty.

What a marvelous turnaround! Not only had a surplus been successfully unloaded, but a profit had been made in the process. Letters flowed in thanking the company for Kleenex Kerchiefs. There were also complaints. It seems that women were not happy that their men were using Kleenex Kerchiefs to blow their noses, and the men wanted to know why it had to be just a woman's product. From a public survey, it was discovered that 60 percent of people were buying Kleenex Kerchiefs for their noses only. Taking advantage of this knowledge, Kleenex Kerchiefs became just Kleenex and was now marketed as a nose-blowing tissue.

What a journey: from wounds to gas masks to faces to just noses. Kleenex demonstrates a classic lesson in the ability to adapt an existing product to a changing market. By not restricting themselves with tunnel vision that could see only the original purpose for their product, the company was able to maintain an open eye and discover new ways of using their product. A willingness to adapt products, careers, skills, and attitudes can literally be the difference between tremendous prosperity or bulging warehouses filled with wasted ingenuity.

Application

A few tips:

1 You are likely working in an organization that deals with a product or service. Mentally review the evolution of that product or service.

2 How versatile has the product or service become? Could it be expanded or adapted further?

3 Brainstorm additional uses by breaking down the marketplace into consumer groups, lifestyle changes, and technology breakthroughs. "Imagine and adapt" should be your mantra.

A willingness to adapt can mean the difference between prosperity and failure.

Lesson 38
Only One Winner?

W E ALL begin learning a certain lesson when we are very young. There are many ways to express this lesson, but perhaps American race car driver Dale Earnhardt said it best: "Second place is just the first loser." Like it or not, we've all been conditioned to believe that there can be only one winner. Unfortunately, this mindset can be very limiting.

If there is one sand pail and two children, only one ends up with the pail. Only one team can win the World Cup or the Super Bowl. If one is a winner, then the other must be ... that ugly word ... the *loser*. It is natural, then, that we spend our time and energy trying to ensure that we will be the winners, and others the losers.

But this needn't be the case. Consider the following: several children were playing near an abandoned railroad track. They were having a contest to see who could balance and walk the farthest without falling off the rail.

After the children made several attempts, two of the girls bet the others that they could walk the entire length of the track without falling off. The boys laughed and eagerly took them up on the bet. Then the two girls mounted opposite rails, leaned into each other, clasped hands for balance, and easily walked the entire length.

So it is with the adult world. Too many of us assume that for us to succeed, someone else must fail. This attitude leads to counterproductive internal rivalries, which may bleed the life out of an organization. Replace internal competition with mutually beneficial and encouraging cooperation, and focus your competitive energies and resources outside the company where they are truly needed.

Eliminate the notion that there must be one winner and all the rest losers. Like the girls on the railroad track, find the win-win solution and extend a supporting arm to those who work with you. You will help yourself, your team, department, organization, and company in the process. The final result may blow the *real* competition out of the water.

Application

A few tips:

1 Yes, occasional internal rivalries and competition can be productive—to a point. But it must never overshadow the emphasis of directing necessary energy and resources outside, in the marketplace.

2 Your primary competition should be directed at your competitors.

3 Think of additional internal alliances and support networks that build and strengthen your organization from within. Help them feel united.

4 Make everyone on your team a winner.

Replace internal competition with mutually beneficial and encouraging cooperation.

Lesson 39
Busy as a Bee

Related Leadership Dimensions
Strategic Thinking
Team Building
Dependability
Inspiring Commitment
Focusing on Results

THE HONEY bee is a legendary symbol of industry and hard work. How we admire its diligence in flying from flower to flower searching for pollen! Its energy is unending as it races to complete its task.

For generations, the marvelous, hardworking honey bee has been held as an example of hard work and industry. It symbolizes diligent labor. It never deviates from its task, never slows down, never falters. It knows what it must do, and it does it.

We admire the student or child who is referred to as being "busy as a bee." We encourage and respect the people who efficiently complete their daily tasks. A person who is observed as always busy at work is regarded as a productive worker.

The worker bee is driven by one goal: securing pollen for the hive. Its whole existence is based on fulfilling that mission. What dedication, what energy, what devotion to the queen bee! Sounds like a great employee. The bee never questions, never varies. He is even willing to risk his life if an enemy impedes his path. What more could an employer want? What a dream to have a worker who does everything they are asked and never questions. A perfect employee—right? Think again.

How do you, as a leader, balance consistent execution of tasks with improvement and innovation? How do you encourage healthy pushback in company policies, procedures, and tasks? How do you promote an honest desire to know "why?"

Enabling employees to voice their concerns as well as their ideas for improvement makes them stronger and more productive. Their department flourishes as a result. But that's not all. The entire organization benefits by having more knowledgeable and creative inputs as well as energized, appreciated, and focused employees!

An environment defined by open, informed two-way communication will generate a fully engaged and committed workforce.

Application

Ask yourself:

1 Are your people free to question policies, procedures, and direction?

2 Do you encourage them to share their concerns?

3 Being busy as a bee seems ideal, but what happens if a major change needs to take place? Your people will adapt if there is open two-way communication so everyone feels included.

Don't be too quick to encourage your employees to imitate the bee. Enable them to voice their concerns as well as their creative ideas.

Lesson 40
The Miracle of the Polaroid

Related Leadership Dimensions
Innovation
Problem Solving
Organizational Savvy
Coaching

OR YEARS, a camera captured pictures on film. The pictures could not be seen until the film was developed. Then a new camera was introduced that allowed users to see pictures within seconds of when they were taken. Even though that technology has been eclipsed by digital technologies, it remains a novel application—not a contradiction—of the rules of film developing.

How does it work? A carefully prepared process is housed in each frame of a pack of film so that individual pictures can be developed as desired. The rules of photography are upheld, but they have been rearranged in a distinctively creative way.

The need of the previously required darkroom to develop the film is satisfied by a chemical coating of an opacifier dye over the picture to protect it from light exposure. To reverse the light protection when the picture is fully developed, alkaline chemicals are released. The law of color development is maintained by mixing the primary colors of red, yellow, and blue. Dye developers released onto the film allow colors to appear and to be immobilized as needed. All this innovation and creativity, along with several new compounds developed just for this film, combine to create the miracle called instant photography.

Polaroid film works within a contained set of rules but still allows flexibility. It is not restrained by strict regulations but instead gives each picture the capability to develop in its own creative sphere. Every picture follows the same developing procedure, but in its own individual way. A good team will capture the picture from the "Polaroid Miracle" and learn the difference between developing and regulating.

"Following the rules" does not mean that your group should be restricted to merely creating old copies using old established rules and traditions. Instead, your team needs to see beyond the traditional. Polaroid took an entirely new approach that still follows the traditional "rules" of developing film. Lead your teammates to a new level of innovation. Help them break the mold. A successful team is not afraid to rearrange the rules to allow freedom for the miracle of innovation.

Application

A few tips:

1 Consider the current set of unwritten and accepted rules that seem to govern your organization.

2 Notice the unspoken barriers and limitations that restrict new ideas.

3 Encourage your team to break out of the old molds by looking at new patterns and combinations. This will allow you to begin your path toward new discoveries.

Do not be afraid to rearrange the rules to allow freedom for the miracle of innovation.

Lesson 41
The Frogs and Fighting Bulls

ONE OF Aesop's fables tells the story of two bulls who were intensely fighting in a field. At one side of the field was a marsh where two frogs lived. The older frog started to tremble as he watched the fierce battle. The younger frog asked, "What are you afraid of? Their quarrel does not impact us."

"Do you not see," replied the old frog, "that the bull who loses that battle will be driven away from the good grass up there to the reeds of this marsh? He will then trample us into the mud!"

It turned out that the old frog was right. The beaten bull was driven to the marsh, where his great hoofs crushed the frogs to death.

In this fable, we see a good leader in action. We are never isolated from the activities of our neighbors, especially in the world of business. What other groups do affects us, either immediately or eventually. A wise leader will be on the watch for these changes and actions, be they large or small, subtle or obvious.

If our friend the frog had been occupying his time entirely with personally monitoring everything his fellow frogs did in the marsh, he would never have had the time to raise his head and see the trouble that would impact his entire group.

Wise leaders recognize the value of freeing up some of their time for the purpose of observing general trends and changes in the field. By delegating daily tasks and allowing team members the freedom to deal with the details, leaders free themselves to observe and study the big picture. And this is where human leaders take it even further than the unfortunate frogs: their efforts are then spent focusing on what is critical and guiding the team accordingly.

Being small or out of the way doesn't completely insulate you from large changes and events. Don't adopt a "swamp" mentality. Stay alert to the whole picture. Your survival and success depend on it.

Application

Pay close attention to what is happening in the marketplace— to trends in technology, the actions of your competitors, and the impact of new products and services. These will eventually affect you. Don't be reactive. Your future depends on it. Ask yourself:

1 What things can you do to free yourself more so you can monitor the issues in the "surrounding pasture"? Can you appreciate how they will impact your group?

2 How much do you delegate to trusted associates who will focus "down and in" while you are focusing "up and out"? This is particularly important for CEOs, presidents, and senior executives.

Use your time and resources to stay alert to the whole picture and how it might affect you and your organization.

Lesson 42
The Right Job, Done Right

Related Leadership Dimensions
Focusing on Results
Strategic Thinking
Time Management
Decision Making
Personal Integrity

OES YOUR neighborhood have a friendly old man who is like a grandfather to all the kids on the street? When I was young, I had such a neighbor. He was kind to all the children. He taught us how to enjoy working. We watched him garden and care for his lawn. His yard was immaculate. His garage was painted inside and covered with pegboards so that every tool was hanging in its proper place. He swept and polished the concrete floor regularly, and then painted it. It was so clean you could eat off of it.

As small children, we followed him around the yard while he mowed his lawn. When he was done, he would trim the edges with scissors. Then, while we watched in amazement, he would place the lawnmower on two sawhorses, crawl underneath in his pressed coveralls, and chisel out all the soggy grass that was underneath. Then he would hose it out and use his air compressor to blow dry the mower.

I once asked him what he did before he retired. He told me with great pride that during the 1940s and 1950s he worked as an efficiency expert. I asked him what that meant. "Efficiency," he said, "is doing the job right."

Sometimes we mistakenly think efficiency means doing the job faster, but faster is not efficient when quality suffers. My dad's mantra was, "Any job worth doing is worth doing right." But that also means that not all jobs are worth doing. The wrong job, no matter how efficiently done, is still a waste of time.

Efficiency is not productive unless it is accompanied by effectiveness. I remember hearing my professor Peter Drucker teaching us: "Efficiency is doing the job right. Effectiveness is doing the right job."

Sometimes we are so involved in getting the job done that we fail to ask if it is the right job to do. It may end up being the right job, but is this the best time to do it? Are there other tasks to be done first? Should it be modified in light of new data or market trends? These are critical questions that should be asked before a job is begun.

Don't become a prisoner to habit and tradition. Of course, we want to be efficient, but let's be effective first. Let's make sure we're doing the right job, and then do it right.

Application

Take a moment to think about typical jobs or tasks you do. Ask yourself:

1 Are they done because of traditional practices?

2 Can you see how habit and routine can keep you too busy to question if there is a better way?

3 How can you make sure the tasks you are doing are the best use of your time?

4 Can you think of new questions you can ask yourself or others that will help your organization be more effective?

Make sure you are doing the right job, and then do it right.

Lesson 43
Taking the Heat

Related Leadership Dimensions
Problem Solving
Personal Development
Innovation
Focusing on Results
Change Management

THE DESERT is a world of extremes. During the day it endures scorching heat, and at night temperatures descend below freezing. There is very little rainfall, so the land and its inhabitants must endure long stretches of time without water. Sounds pretty uninhabitable.

Many plants and animals, however, thrive in this extreme environment. To survive, many desert animals have discovered vital secrets we can learn from.

The camel prepares for famine by storing up during an occasional feast. As it eats, a portion of its food is transformed into fat. The fat is stored in the top of the camel's back—the hump. The camel drinks up to twenty-five gallons of water at one time, because it will likely be a long time before water is available again.

Most desert animals learn to adjust their sleeping schedules to take advantage of the chilly hours. When the heat is the hottest, they burrow into the cooler ground and sleep. Their breathing helps keep their abodes moist. Some animals even stay asleep for days at a time during severe heat waves.

Most hunting is done at night. With extra-large ears, a fox can detect its prey even in the dark. Some animals, like the addax, do not need water but get their liquid from plants that store water in their leaves. Others, like wallabies and kangaroos, provide their own air conditioning by washing their bodies in their saliva.

The animals are equipped with skills that help them utilize their environment and prepare for the harsh conditions they face. They have learned to "take the heat" and deal with it in a successful way.

In many of our "hot" times, there is nothing we can do to reduce the heat or remove ourselves from the situation. We must learn to adapt our behavior to live within it the best we can. Not one of the animals mentioned ever thought of how to escape, but instead they adapted their energies to make the most of their environment. They have succeeded in spite of immense odds. Consider adopting the same attitude toward your environment—no matter how unpleasant or demanding it seems to be.

Think of ways you can adapt your schedule and lifestyle to better utilize the positive aspects of your environment, whether it be work, school, or home. Identify the challenges you face. Be creative in seeking ways you can adjust your limitations, work space, or efforts to overcome those challenges. "Take the heat" and transform it into a source of positive energy for yourself and those around you.

Application

Here are some points for reflection.

1 What are some work-specific conditions you must face that are difficult to deal with?

2 Think of ways you can better adapt your preferences and customary behaviors to them.

3 In doing so, you may find that you discover new and better alternatives, compatibilities, or modifications to your regular habits.

4 In the end, you will likely see a better, more productive attitude in yourself because of your positive responsiveness.

When the heat is on, how can you turn it into a source of positive energy and an opportunity to succeed?

Lesson 44
Harmonic Persistence

Related Leadership Dimensions
Innovation
Personal Development
Inspiring Commitment
Time Management
Coaching

LECK WAS born into a wealthy, famous family. It would have been easy for him to just hide under the family security blanket and follow in the footsteps of his illustrious relatives. To Aleck, that was not an alternative he could live with. At the age of eleven, Alexander Graham Bell began to forge his own life.

To Graham, as he preferred to be called, he could no more stop inventing than he could stop eating. The search for answers to questions was a calling he could not avoid. To some, this was a quality greatly criticized by others—investigating things of interest without seeming to accomplish much—but for Graham, this dominant trait led to remarkable success later in life.

The quest that held the most interest for Alexander Graham Bell was the search for a means of transmitting vibrations from one location to another. His mother and wife were deaf from childhood accidents, so the transmission of sound through the use of vibration was very important to him. He referred to this dream as his "harmonic telegraph." He realized that he alone did not possess all the knowledge necessary, so he acquired the help of a brilliant young electrician named Tom Watson. Together, they would perform the "miracle heard round the world."

In the time preceding this miraculous discovery, Graham continued to teach and lecture as he pursued his dream. There was much room for doubt and discouragement as critics belittled Bell and Watson for attempting something so utterly ludicrous. Even Bell himself began to doubt a bit. But as he later wrote, "It is easier for an inventor to stop breathing than to discontinue trying." His diligence finally paid off, and with the majestic refrain of "God Save the Queen" and the simple greeting, "How do you do?" the first telephone was born. Alexander Graham Bell was a man who knew what he wanted out of life and went after it relentlessly.

Ask yourself: What drives or motivates you? Is your job aligned with your career and life goals? How do you stay on track despite setbacks? What is your level of persistence and tenacity? Aligning your day-to-day activities with your long-term objectives will increase your productivity and happiness. You may not be driven to invent, but staying focused on what motivates you and your people will bring about a harmonic and productive persistence—and your entire organization will benefit!

Application

Here are some points for consideration.

1 Are you meeting many of your life goals and dreams?

2 What are some of the barriers you are bumping into that impede your progress?

3 Just as Graham teamed up with Watson, consider partnering with a colleague to accomplish specific goals.

4 Try to alter some of your daily or weekly schedules to allow small chunks of time for working on particularly satisfying activities that you have been forced to delay.

Despite setbacks, stay focused on what motivates you.

Lesson 45
How Far Would You Go?

Related Leadership Dimensions
Personal Integrity
Valuing Others
Inspiring Commitment
Innovation
Personal Development

THERE WAS a young girl who always dreamed of getting a formal education so she could grow and reach her life's full potential. Her father was a teacher and she dreamed of becoming a teacher as well. However, in her village and country, this was not encouraged or even accepted for women. Her father believed in her but warned that to pursue this path could be dangerous.

Against all odds, this courageous girl persisted with her dream. She went to school and encouraged other young girls to go to school. At age twelve, using social media, she began to speak out about how all women should be given this right to an education. Her activities were even more courageous given the frequent military conflicts around her.

After about two years of her social activism, she was awarded her country's first youth peace prize, as well as receiving a nomination for an international peace prize. This brought added attention to her identity and efforts. Consequently, she was targeted by an extremist faction. One day as she was heading home from school, a man boarded her bus, asked for her by name, and fired a single shot at her head.

Now a familiar figure, Malala Yousafzai, the young woman from Pakistan who miraculously survived and became a symbol for human rights around the globe, eventually became the youngest recipient of the Noble Peace Prize.

How far would you go to stand up for what you believe in? Would you have the courage to uphold your beliefs and convictions even if they go against popular or accepted practices? Malala's example serves as a powerful symbol of resilient determination and integrity.

Application

Here are a few points for reflection:

1 Lead by example, because others watch and will model your behavior.

2 If your organization has a written code of values or ethics, find it, learn it, and be true to it. If not, start one of your own.

3 Don't ignore an unethical situation, as this will create the impression that you condone it.

4 Foster trust by establishing honest and open communication within all your relationships.

5 Create an environment in which people feel safe to come to you with their concerns. Honor their confidence.

How far would you go to stand up for what you believe in?

Lesson 46
The Nose Knows

W ITH AWKWARD splats and swishes, the furry, brown creature works its way through the water. Sifting mud with its snout, it struggles hard to find its dinner. Its favorite dishes are tadpoles, earthworms, and shellfish, which can all be found on the banks of freshwater rivers.

When early colonizers in Australia sent a platypus pelt back to England, scientists there thought the animal was an elaborate hoax—even checking for signs of stitches, thinking someone had sewn various animals together. The platypus has webbed feet like a duck, a tail like a beaver, a squatty body with short front legs, and a long, rubbery snout. How could an animal such as this survive, let alone flourish?

When a platypus dives to find its next meal, it closes its eyes, ears, and nose—so how does it find anything? The platypus is the only mammal known to have the use of electroreception. Its nose, or bill, has electroreceptors that can detect tiny electrical currents generated by its prey. These receptors are so sensitive they have been known to differentiate "artificial shrimp" from real shrimp based on their generated electrical currents.

This strange and unusual creature is a marvelous example of leveraging all of one's assets for maximum advantage. Rather than bemoaning its highly unconventional collection of attributes, it has chosen to use them to its benefit. Ignoring its patchwork outward appearance, it concentrates on enhancing the strengths it has. Learning to combine its unusual qualities has created a specialized set of skills unique to the platypus. It has learned not just to rely on what it sees or hears, but also to trust its nose. In the murky water it could easily be tricked into seeing something in a distorted way. Learning to trust the information it receives through its electroreceptors, it can discover the true picture. The platypus' nose knows.

Regardless of how unconventional your skill set may be, or the challenging situations you face, adapting and developing strengths can lead to increased capabilities. In fact, your "unconventional" skill set may be exactly what your challenges call for.

Consider making a list of strengths for you and your team. Identify how these strengths can be leveraged to accomplish current and future work needs. Learn to rely on these strengths. Champion the unique assets of others. The combination will lead to the achievement of remarkable or unconventional outcomes.

Application

Think of how often you have disparaged some of your features or capabilities because they are outside the norm. Consider:

1 Looking at one unusual or unconventional attribute alone may cause you despair. But combining it with others will likely allow you to accomplish surprising results.

2 View others through the same lens. Combine their non-traditional abilities with those of others on the team. The outcome may be very satisfying.

Your "unconventional" skill set may be exactly what your challenges call for.

Lesson 47
Snake and Eggs

Related Leadership Dimensions
Personal Development
Coaching
Delegating
Inspiring Commitment

A LOT CAN be learned from the attitude of a snake.

Have you ever seen one eat an object larger than its own diameter? Look at a great big egg, and a small snake, and skeptically say: "There's no way that skinny snake can swallow such a large egg."

But nobody told the snake it couldn't do it. Watch as it slowly but methodically opens its mouth wider and wider and then begins to stretch it over the top of the egg. Now your initial doubts are waning. You think, "Well, maybe it just might..." and with amazement you watch the egg slowly disappear inside its mouth. Then its slim body expands to accommodate the unnatural bulge.

A manager, confronted with delegating a challenge, will look at an employee and say, "There's no way Jim can handle this task. I'd better do it myself." If the manager is wise, she will avoid this first impulse and give Jim the opportunity to try. Just like the snake, if Jim is truly motivated, if he is given confidence in his abilities, and is provided support and guidance from his leader, he will likely *stretch* to meet the daunting challenge.

The snake really wanted the egg and was willing to commit itself completely to the task. Our slithery friend felt confident that it could do it and didn't stop until the job was done. A big jump for a manager is letting go and allowing others to try. They may fail, but they will learn from it and try again.

However, there is a danger. If, for example, a snake attempts to swallow a large toad starting from the toad's rear instead of the front, the toad's legs likely will get stuck, preventing the snake from completely swallowing. Since the snake's teeth are angled back sharply, it cannot let go of the toad, and may die.

Likewise, employees with a major challenge and no aid can end up choking. Don't abandon them. Know their tendencies and be available for help. Teach them how to approach the task properly, and give them appropriate coaching and support without smothering them, so that they don't choke. In the end, both you and your employees will share a marvelous feeling of victory and personal fulfillment when the challenging task has been completed, and you both agree that, "Yes, it can be done, and we did it!"

Application

A few tips:

1 Learn from your own experiences of being on the receiving end of delegated tasks.

2 Ponder recent tasks that you delegated to others. Who received them? How difficult were they? What type of support did you provide?

3 Employees can sense the amount of confidence you have in them when you delegate. This is obvious by the way you present the task.

4 Be available to guide them through the delegated assignment if they need help, but avoid smothering them.

"Yes, it can be done."

Lesson 48
The Roots of a Giant

Related Leadership Dimensions
Team Building
Ego Management
Valuing Others
Organizational Savvy
Change Management

OHN MUIR, a Scottish-born American naturalist and conservationist, wrote of the giant sequoia: "Behold! Behold! seems all I can say." Anyone who has stood at the base of these awe-inspiring giants knows just what he meant. How can so grand a creation be called a mere tree? The tallest of these reach over three hundred feet into the sky and many can boast a circumference of over one hundred feet. It is not just their size that inspires, but also their longevity. The oldest living sequoia is 3,300 years old. They are resistant to disease, fire, fungi, and insects. Indeed, these trees seem invincible.

Of all the amazing features of the sequoia, its root system is perhaps the most impressive and baffling. As it grows, it spreads its roots far and wide—sometimes two hundred to three hundred feet in every direction, but not deep. Sequoias never develop a deep or permanent taproot. Their entire root system is generally only about six feet below the surface of the earth. It seems completely improbable that such a shallow root system could support so massive a tree.

This shallow yet extensive root network allows sequoias to live and grow to incredible heights without overconsuming the nutrients in the soil. In fact, sequoias develop a very stable, long-term relationship with the soil around them. Researchers have found that from year to year the soil around these trees maintains consistent levels of all the minerals, moisture, and nutrients needed to sustain them.

Interestingly, most of their initial growth is focused in the roots, with little visible evidence of increased size. Only after the root system is in place does the tree begin significant upward growth.

The root system responds to change very effectively. Rising groundwater levels brought on by floods that frequently "drown" trees with deep roots have no negative impact on the sequoia. The tree simply produces a new lateral root system. If the tree sustains damage and begins leaning in one direction, the roots respond by strengthening the opposing side of the tree to restore balance.

Think of your organization. Do you assume that the greatness of your organization lies in its lofty top branches? How much time and energy are expended on developing the root system? Do you recognize your dependence on the vast network of people who form the foundation of all you do? Do you respond well to changes in your environment—changes that these individuals, the roots, generally notice long before the *upper branches*? Changes that the roots are generally better able to respond to? Remember: you need vital organizational roots. No one can do it all alone, not even a giant.

Application

A few tips:

1 Recognize the fundamental role that *all* levels of the organization play in its vital functions—especially the "roots." Appreciate and acknowledge them often.

2 Adapt to both planned and unplanned changes by making necessary adjustments. This is especially true in the value and role of the root system.

3 The stronger and more cared for the base of the organization is, the sturdier and taller it will grow.

4 You can *never* make it by yourself.

You need your "roots." No one can do it all alone, not even a giant.

Lesson 49
Tuning In to Crickets

TWO MEN were walking along a crowded sidewalk in a downtown business area. Suddenly one exclaimed, "Listen to the lovely sound of that cricket." But the other could not hear it. He asked his companion how he could detect the sound of a cricket amid the din of people and traffic. The first man, who was a zoologist, had trained himself to listen to the voices of nature. But he didn't explain. He simply took a coin out of his pocket and dropped it to the sidewalk, whereupon a dozen people began to look about them. "We hear," he said, "what we listen for."

This story, attributed to Dr. Kermit Long, illustrates a weakness that can limit our effectiveness and create artificial "boxes" that keep us thinking and acting in the same old ways. If we train ourselves not to hear certain input, such as negative feedback, constructive criticism, or ideas that seem threatening, we will eventually become completely deaf to them by choice. We will consequently lose many opportunities for personal growth and professional progress.

As leaders, what do we listen for? Have we trained ourselves to really listen to our people? Or do we tune in to only the messages we want to hear? Do we listen to what is important to them, or only to messages we think are important to us?

Listening is hard work, but it is the easiest way to let someone know you sincerely care. Without it you cannot learn what you need to know. Listening allows you to tune in to the concerns, frustrations, emotional changes, and whims of your employees, customers, suppliers, and vendors. It dramatically increases your responsiveness to them and their needs. Genuine listening is a gift of time.

To really listen, you must want to hear the message. Effective listening means not only hearing what people say, but also understanding their intended meaning. This requires much more than merely waiting for someone to finish speaking. Improved listening skills will enhance your interpersonal capabilities, your relationships (personal and professional), all your communications, and your selling and negotiating abilities. It is the keystone of your people skills. In fact, the person who listens with understanding is also the one who eventually is the most listened to.

Like the man who heard the cricket, tune in to those who work with you. You will be amazed by what you learn, and by what good listening will accomplish in strengthening relationships and increasing productivity.

Application

A few tips:

1 Consider any relationships you have that need improving. Enhanced listening skills will improve them dramatically.

2 When you listen, focus more on what is being said than on your response. Too often, people just "wait out" the speaker so they can then interject with their own opinions.

3 Listening allows you to learn far more than speaking does.

4 When you listen properly, you learn.

"We hear what we listen for."

Lesson 50
Sixty-Five Years Young

Related Leadership Dimensions
Change Management
Personal Development
Innovation
Inspiring Commitment
Coaching

ARLAND HAD lived a life full of hard work and hard times, but had little to show for it by his sixty-fifth birthday. His father had died when he was just five years old. His mom went to work, and Harland took on the responsibility of cooking and caring for his family. When his mom remarried, Harland ran away from home and joined the US Army. After his service, he held many jobs to provide for his family.

He worked tirelessly, but never excelled in those jobs, and none lasted long.

Then, at the age of forty, he started cooking for hungry travelers at a service station. He didn't have a restaurant, so he served people in his living quarters. Using an old family recipe and the cooking skills he gained as a young man, he prepared Southern comfort food for the travelers. His reputation as a chef and the popularity of his meals grew until he was able to expand the business to a motel and a restaurant that seated 142 people. For many years, his restaurant, Court & Cafe, was successful, but even with all his effort and popularity, the cards were stacked against him. The construction of the interstate highway and the subsequent reduction in customer traffic forced him out of business and left him nearly penniless.

On the day he closed the Court & Cafe, he received his first Social Security check, for $105. Fortunately, Harland had seen the potential to franchise his old family recipe and his image. Three years earlier, he had established his first franchise in Salt Lake City, Utah. But this one franchise wasn't much and there were barriers to overcome if other franchises were to follow. At sixty-five, these were daunting challenges.

Harland took that $105 and hit the road. He traveled from town to town cooking food and seeking potential franchise owners. Success didn't come overnight; Harland had to work hard and seek help from successful restaurateurs. But five years later, the "Kentucky Colonel" and his "finger-lickin' good" chicken were found in four hundred locations in the United States and Canada. The business continued to grow and Harland, or Colonel Sanders as most people knew him, finally achieved the success he had worked so hard for all his life.

There is no expiration date on our ability to succeed. Hard work pays off, even if it takes a while for the "check" to come. Failures, handled well, may just pave the way to future—and greater—success. Challenges (like having to drop out of school and cook for your family) are often the greatest blessings and opportunities in our lives. All of these lessons are things Colonel Sanders might tell us, if he were here.

Application

Here are some points to consider.

1 The keys to Colonel Sanders' success were determination and hard work. Nothing worthwhile comes easily.

2 Note his many failures and setbacks. In spite of these, he kept trying.

3 Colonel Sanders sought the wisdom and advice of others and learned from them.

4 All of the above apply to each of us in our pursuit of our dreams.

There is no expiration date on our ability to succeed.

Lesson 51
Fantastic or a Flop?

Related Leadership Dimensions
Personal Development
Focusing on Results
Problem Solving
Innovation
Coaching

N 1968, sports history was made. A young man by the name of Dick Fosbury was able to clear the high jump at a record-setting height of seven feet, four and a quarter inches (2.24 meters). He set an Olympic record and received the acclaim of the world for his accomplishment. Though the record height alone is worthy of praise, it is the method Dick used that brings the most admiration and attention.

When Dick began his jumping career, he watched and learned from the big boys on his high school team and later his college teammates. He carefully tried to emulate their style and improve his own skills, although somehow it didn't feel right when he tried their method of jumping. He experimented with other styles until he finally developed for himself a strange, funny sort of "flop over the bar" kind of jump. When he used it he was able to leap much higher than when he used the traditional methods. It was a very awkward-looking jump and it was not approved of by Dick's coaches. They criticized him endlessly and tried to steer him away from this funny "flopping" jump style.

But Dick knew he was right. As he said, "I didn't change my style. It changed me." He continued to develop this new approach contrary to the advice of his coaches. It was not until he began to clear seven feet at a regular rate that the coaches started to relent and believe in Dick's strange style. The rest is history. Not only did Dick Fosbury go on to make world record-breaking jumps, but he also changed the entire high jumping methodology. His Fosbury Flop, as his jump style is now called, is the most popular and successful jumping style in the event.

Each of us has a style all our own. Sometimes it is not "traditional" and we have to fight against the criticism of our coaches. Don't change the style that is the essence of who you are. *You know you the best.* Study and analyze your current and potential talents and inclinations. Mold and develop these into a style of working that you are comfortable with, that is natural to you, and that produces the results you seek. Listen, watch, and learn all you can. Practice diligently. But with all that hard work, be true to what is you. Let your style change you, and you will qualify to stand with the best.

Application

A few tips:

1 Observe, study, and learn from others who excel in your chosen field. Note the skills that lead them to successes.

2 Know your own tendencies, talents, and skills. Mold these into your style to help you improve your performance in sport, at home, or at work.

3 Pay attention to your "coaches," but be true to yourself. The result of your own performance is the real test.

4 The techniques and methods of the past are often replaced by new ones. Be a pioneer and explore breakthroughs in your field.

Your style is your own. Don't worry if it's not traditional; it is right for you.

Lesson 52
What Makes a Symphony?

Related Leadership Dimensions
Strategic Thinking
Team Building
Effective Communication
Focusing on Results
Ego Management
Listening

WHILE ATTENDING a symphony, it is pretty hard to avoid noticing the conductor. He is the one standing on the platform performing a strange and mysterious arm-waving ritual that somehow tells the musicians how to play. The conductor's style can vary anywhere from restrained to erratic, but still the symphony plays. Is all that arm flailing really necessary?

Regardless of the style, the "arm flailing" is sending an essential message. The musicians in the symphony know what, when, and how to play their parts because of the signals sent by the conductor. They know to watch for the downstroke of the conductor's right hand, indicating the first beat of each measure, and the upstroke, indicating the last beat of the measure. Because the musicians are well trained in their parts, the conductor need not indicate every separate note to be played.

Standing on the platform in full view of all the musicians, the conductor is ready to direct each individual to play as part of a synchronized whole. He has the musical score before him. He sees the big picture and knows when to tone down a section and when to encourage musicians to play louder. He makes movements ranging from short, abrupt strokes to large, powerful waves to interpret the mood of the music. With respect for each musician, and guided by the score prepared by the composer, the conductor carefully blends each individual's instrument together to create a masterful performance.

All the players know their parts well and could probably play just fine without the leader. But without the conductor, their individual parts would never become a *symphony*. A symphony consists of polished performances from many sections that become a unified whole. If not played together, they are merely a cacophony of disconnected sounds. To achieve the intended level of performance, there must be a conductor who has the entire score (not just individual parts) constantly before him, and who blends all the individual parts into one melodic sound. That is the power held in the hand of the conductor.

Leadership is the ability to translate vision into successful reality. The conductor, with the musical score, brings the individual instruments into a harmonized whole. Leaders must see the "big picture" to accomplish the same thing with their people. Each leader will apply an individual style, but if the vision is not clearly defined, no amount of charisma or talent will make up for a lack of direction. Only with this clearly communicated perspective from an experienced and wise leader will all the unique, individual parts come together in a magnificent and satisfying performance.

Application

A couple of points for consideration:

1 To succeed in your leadership role, it is vital that you understand and know each of your "players" and their capacity to "play." Only then are you in a position to "direct" all of them to produce a successful and satisfying performance.

2 As with a great conductor, make sure you are certain of the direction your team needs to go. Only when this is clear are you in a position to "conduct" them to that end.

Only a clearly communicated perspective, directed by a wise and capable leader, results in a magnificent performance.

Acknowledgments

OVER THE years, I have traveled the globe working with leaders in countless varieties of challenges. I dedicate these Lessons to those thousands of leaders who have shown me that leadership can be taught and learned, thereby achieving extraordinarily satisfying results through others. They have demonstrated my philosophy that the only way you can succeed is by helping your people succeed.

There are many who have supported and encouraged me in my research, consulting, and coaching over the years. These include my clients, staff, editors, friends, associates, and family.

In particular, I salute and honor my wife for her sustaining and constant support, encouragement, and patience with my crazy schedule, work, travel, and research. To Debra, I give my love and gratitude.

I also express appreciation to our four sons—Daniel, Peter, Jared, and Brian—for their always-willing, drop-of-a-hat support for anything I ever needed. My son Daniel was an exceptional writing partner through the entire process. It was a father's joy to have such a privilege.

I offer my sincere appreciation to my clients for the experiences they have given me in the role of "laboratory," allowing me to experiment and test my theories—usually successfully.

Some of the most satisfying learning and associations came from my consulting, teaching, and coaching opportunities with:

- Lockheed Martin—thirteen years in developing, designing, and teaching the Lockheed Martin Executive Institutes. CEOs Roy Anderson and Dan Tellep, you are class acts!

- NASA—twelve years in teaching the leaders of Kennedy Space Center, who achieved an award fee score of 100 for the first time in their history. Well done, Jay Honeycutt! What challenges—both tragic and joyful—we witnessed and overcame!

- Toshiba, and the unique executive training sessions we had in the classroom and mountains with you, Tom Leavitt.

- Telstra—Sydney and Melbourne—Coaching the Executive Leadership Programs.

- United Space Alliance—working with CEO Kent Black and COO Jim Adamson in developing their executive team in the early years of the Lockheed Martin, Rockwell, Boeing venture.

- CSL-Hong Kong—coaching and training Tarek Robbiati's senior team. What a pleasure to coach your team individually and collectively as we had off-site meetings in China and Macau. You guys sure knew these Lessons!

- Pacific Bell (Verizon)—coaching and training all managers in network engineering and sales for three years. Chuck Hensley, we made a huge difference!

* Idaho National Engineering Lab—five years in coaching and developing all of management as they experienced major change initiatives. Beth Britt, it was a genuine pleasure!

* Johnson Space Center in Houston—simultaneously working with every major contractor in supporting the shuttle operations. Bill Brett of Raytheon, what a time we had!

* US Department of Agriculture National Agricultural Statistics Service—coaching and executive development with the SES Team. Dr. Clark, you had more challenges thrown at you than any previous administrator!

* National Institute for Internal Auditors—Training and Developing Leadership Skills. Those weekly sessions were long and tough, but so worth it!

I sincerely thank Ken Shelton and Allan Jensen for their tireless and patient help, support, knowledge, experience, judgment, and professionalism in editing the first edition of this book. It was a pleasure to work with them and Leadership Excellence as we completed and published the original version of this book. They were always encouraging and most helpful in countless ways!

Finally, to my highly skilled and very capable in-house editors, Peter Stewart and Megan Wilcken, as well as to the professional support at Page Two: I acknowledge all your work with my highest praise and appreciation. You made it happen!

Index

Index by leadership dimension (in alphabetical order)

The following index is organized by the four quadrants of the LEAD NOW! Model and the 21 Leadership Dimensions. The Leadership Lessons are listed under the dimensions to which they relate. Connecting the Leadership Lessons to the LEAD NOW! Model will help you develop a personal comprehensive leadership development strategy.

Customer Focus (Create Purpose)

Decision Making (Deliver Excellence)

Delegating (Deliver Excellence)

Dependability (Deliver Excellence)

Effective Communication (Create Purpose)

Ego Management (Develop Self & Others)

Focusing on Results (Deliver Excellence)

About the Author

JOHN PARKER Stewart is the founder and CEO of Stewart Leadership, which he started in 1980. He is globally recognized as a leadership coach, consultant, educator, speaker, and team performance specialist. Under his guidance, Stewart Leadership is recognized internationally for its feedback assessments, training tools, and solid, results-focused coaching services designed to help teams and individuals adapt, grow, and reach new levels of performance. John has coached and trained tens of thousands of leaders worldwide, including CEOs, presidents, military, government, and business leaders, resulting in significant, measured improvement in individual and team performance.

John began his career overseeing leadership and management development for 86,000 employees at Lockheed Corporation. He was awarded the title of National Trainer of the Year by the American Society for Training & Development. In addition to training and coaching all levels of management at Kennedy Space Center over an eight-year period during the high-pressure space shuttle program, John has worked with Citibank, Chevron, Lockheed Martin, Toshiba, CSL-Hong Kong, Xerox, GM, Kaiser Permanente, Telstra, the

US Department of Energy, Shell, and other government agencies and commercial firms.

John has published several articles, manuals, workbooks, and the three-book award-winning Stewart Leadership Series. The first edition of his title book, *LEAD NOW! A Personal Leadership Coaching Guide for Results-Driven Leaders*, won the National Indie Excellence Award for the best leadership book published over the last five years. His *52 Leadership Lessons* is also nationally recognized. John's latest book is titled *Mastering the Art of Oral Presentations*, published by John Wiley & Sons. This book is an essential tool for teams seeking to win government contracts, as well as a valuable guide for presenters in any field.

John lives with his wife, Debra, near Portland, Oregon, and has four sons and sixteen grandchildren.